KU-789-029

S K I L F U L

A TRACK
THLETICS

Nick Whitehead

A & C Black · London

First published 1990 by
A & C Black (Publishers) Limited
35 Bedford Row, London WC1R 4JH

© Nick Whitehead 1990

ISBN 0 7136 5759 6

All rights reserved. No part of this publication
may be reproduced, stored in a retrieval system,
or transmitted in any form or by any means,
electronic, mechanical, photocopying, recording
or otherwise, without the prior permission in
writing of A & C Black (Publishers) Limited.

A CIP catalogue record for this book is
available from the British Library

Acknowledgements
The author and publishers would like to thank the following for their assistance in the
preparation of this book:

Mike Makin
ASICS (Olympian Sports UK Ltd)
All-Sport Photographic Ltd for the cover photograph, the frontispiece photograph and for the
photographs on pages 15 and 46 (left), Eileen Langsley for the photographs on pages 16 and
52; Action-Plus Photographic for the photographs on pages 24, 38, 44, 53 (top), 59, 60, 63
(middle and bottom), 72, 80, and 82; and Photolink (R. and J. Clayton) for the photographs on
pages 17–23, 25, 26, 28, 34, 37, 40–3, 46 (right), 47–51, 53 (bottom), 63 (top), 76, 77 and 84

796.42
WHI

A1 6044
KAB

Typeset by Latimer Trend & Company Ltd, Plymouth
Printed and bound in Great Britain by
William Clowes Limited, Beccles and London

Right **An ecstatic Carl
Lewis after the USA relay
team clinched victory at
the Olympic Games**

CONTENTS

FOREWORD

Nick Whitehead is well qualified to write this authoritative guide to the sport of track athletics. As a sprinter he won bronze medals at both the Olympic and the Commonwealth Games and he was manager of the Great Britain Track and Field Athletics Team at the Moscow and the Los Angeles Olympics.

As well as his vast coaching experience, Nick is able to draw upon the research he undertook during his career in physical education.

Skilful Track Athletics is essential reading for athletes, teachers and coaches. It is thoughtfully set out, with sequential practices, schedules and standards offering the reader a guide to progress.

I strongly recommend this book to all those who are involved in our sport.

Sebastian Coe OBE

INTRODUCTION

Athletes and athletics coaches tend to be very technique-conscious. Coaches often seem to have a picture in their minds of the perfect athlete performing in a perfect fashion, and they direct the athletes in their care to spend hours practising a skill in an attempt to emulate that theoretical image.

Athletes seem not to mind practising these skills, possibly because the amount of effort involved is not very great compared with a hard repetition running session, or a hard weight-training session! But what both athletes and coaches ought to consider is whether all athletes *should* perform in an identical fashion – because athletes are not endowed with identical physiques, skill-learning abilities or temperaments.

Shouldn't the athlete with stronger than average legs aim to use his leg strength? Shouldn't the athlete with the faster leg action aim to use his leg speed? Shouldn't the athlete with the greater arm and shoulder strength use this to his advantage? Shouldn't the coach also take into account the athlete's mental as well as physical qualities?

If we examine the performances of years gone by, we will see that Jesse Owens's 1936 long jump world record of 8.13m was performed in what would be regarded today as a 'very poor style'! Yet this record stood for over thirty years despite improvements in training methods, run-up surfaces, diet, etc. Similarly, many recent world record holders cannot be regarded as prime examples of 'good style', but they have used their own particular abilities and strengths to the full and have beaten others who were better stylists.

This book examines each event, describes what is essential to the mechanically efficient performance of it and, beginning with simple practices, outlines progressive stages through which athletes should practise, becoming accomplished in each before they move on to the next.

Each section begins with a description of the type of athlete likely to succeed in the event named; the equipment needed is described, the progressive stages through which to practise are illustrated, training schedules for the event are itemised and the rules for the event are summarised.

In the Appendices there appear details of performances which beginners in both schools and clubs can aspire to attain.

Note Throughout the book athletes are referred to individually as 'he'. This should, of course, be taken to mean 'he or she' where appropriate.

FITNESS FOR TRACK EVENTS

Often lack of success and even injury can result from athletes practising an event before their bodies are adequately prepared for it. It could be said that they were not 'fit', even though they may have thought they were.

Much progress has been made in recent years in the acquisition of knowledge about the techniques of track events, but astonishingly there is still much confusion about 'fitness' for these events. Not only is there disagreement among coaches as to the best methods of attaining 'fitness', but coaches and athletes use the term in such a fashion that they demonstrate their ignorance of the true fitness needs of the various track events.

In fact, the level of fitness and training needs is different not only for each event, but for each athlete. It is easy to accept that a 'fit' water polo player is not necessarily 'fit' for basketball playing, or that a world record holder in a track event could be regarded as completely 'unfit' in a swimming situation. Yet coaches tend to give all the sprinters in a group the same 'fitness' schedules regardless of their age and ability, ignoring the fact that some of these individuals need to apply more effort than others.

In recent years a wide variety of methods of testing the abilities and fitness levels of athletes have become available. These include physiological testing procedures from the simple pulse rate taking before and after exercise to the computerised treadmill max. VO_2 measurements for top-class athletes.

In addition to the physiological, the very important analysis of technique and style can be quantified, thus illustrating whether or not the force in an athlete's event is being applied in the correct direction. This 'biomechanical' work can also be introduced at a simplified level in clubs by film and video analysis of the athlete. At international level the costly but worthwhile computer-linked film studies can illustrate any incorrect techniques in a three-dimensional form. Many top-class athletes have profited from these sophisticated techniques, and countries realising the gold-medal-winning possibilities have invested vast human and financial resources to enable their Olympic teams to benefit.

Dietary considerations have also become important, and vitamin deficiency and the like are nowadays easily identified by coaches who examine their athletes' regular food intake. Some athletes need to use additives to supplement their food because of their arduous training. These should be taken under medical guidance and should never contain substances banned by world sports authorities.

The importance of the psychological factor is being recognised more and more. Techniques are available to assess athletes' reactions under stress and their will to win. Sports psychologists are becoming more in evidence, both at training camps and accompanying international sports teams.

However, it is not possible within the confined space of this book to deal with all aspects of fitness, namely circulorespiratory endurance, muscular endurance, strength, flexibility and the psychological factors. Readers are therefore recommended to refer for all of this information and the construction of individual fitness programmes to *Conditioning for Sport* (A & C Black, 1988) by this author (see page 94).

WARMING UP AND DOWN

One of the common features in the acquisition of fitness for different track events is a group of activities known as warming up or stretching exercises. These should be carried out prior to engaging in very vigorous activity before both training sessions and competitions.

Different coaches tend to emphasise different benefits to be gained from these exercises, and some athletes disagree with their coaches in their estimation of how valuable the exercises are at all. Nevertheless, the best athletes always warm up before they begin any explosive activity. Some use the exercises to ensure that their muscles are gradually lengthened so that when the track session begins, they do not 'pull' or tear muscles. Others are of the opinion that the stretching exercises ensure a raising of body temperature and pulse rate with a resultant improvement in performance when they begin their track session. Yet others simply use the warm-up period for psychological preparation for the task ahead; they perform mechanically the routine of stretching, while concentrating on a mental rehearsal of the event to come.

Whatever the purpose of the warm-up, the exercises should not be too tiring and should not be spread over too long a period of time, but they should contain a variety that will exercise most of the muscle groups in the body, including the heart and the lungs, and in particular those muscles to be used in the athlete's own event. They should normally be preceded by slow jogging of up to 1,500m, and even in cold climates should not exceed a period of thirty minutes. They will vary according to the athlete's event, age, physiological make-up, the weather, and whether the race is a heat, a semi-final or a final.

Each coach or athlete will develop a group of exercises that have been acquired from experience. Periodically, these exercises should be reviewed and others substituted because an athlete's or coach's favourite routines can neglect important muscle groups. Moreover, using the same exercises for a period of time can result in the athlete not putting in much effort, in which case the exercises will not produce the desired effect.

Immediately after exercise or competition it is also important to warm down. This will be a period of ten minutes or so of jogging and gentle stretching to ensure that the waste products in the muscles do not remain there.

It is appropriate also here to refer to the recent craze for wearing tights in training and competition. In cold climates sensible athletes have always worn tights in the winter to prevent hamstring muscle pulls. However, when athletes such as Florence Griffith-Joyner wear one long leg tight and one short, it has to be asked whether this latest innovation is of any value.

There follow some descriptions of stretching exercises that have been used by top-class athletes.

Exercise 1 (all body)
Trunk rotation

1. After the jogging, the stretching begins with an exercise that uses most of the muscle groups. The athletes, still dressed in track suits or warm clothes, bend down with hands clasped out in front of the body. Feet are shoulder-width apart and knees are not locked.
2. While retaining their balance, the athletes

stretch their arms as far away from the body as possible. It is a slow, sustained movement.

3. Rotating around the waist, the athletes press the arms as far back behind the body as possible without overbalancing. Younger athletes do not have the strength in their abdominal muscles to be able to lean far back.

4. Slowly the arms are swept far to the other side on the way down. On reaching the starting position the exercise is performed in the opposite direction. It can be repeated 6 times or more.

Exercise 2 (legs) Hamstring stretch

1. The athletes begin with legs crossed over so that the outsides of the feet touch. It is a simple stance which children find little problem in adopting.

2. Slowly they attempt to place the palms of their hands on the floor, or touch their toes with their fingers. This must be a gentle stretch. Some athletes will not be able to reach their toes.

3. The athletes then raise their bodies and return to the starting position.

4. So that each group of hamstring muscles is stretched separately, the feet are then changed round and the exercise is repeated in a slow, stretching fashion. About 6 times with each leg in front is an average number to attempt.

Exercise 3 (arms) Arm circle

1. With the palms of the hands on their thighs, the athletes stand lightly on the balls of their feet, with feet shoulder-width apart.

2. The arms are lifted forwards stiffly, straight and very slowly until they are extended high in the air. The arms touch the ears and the body is raised on to the toes.

3. Slowly, the arms are pressed backwards and downwards. A tightness will be felt across the chest and between the shoulder-blades.

4. The arms are lowered to the starting position at the same time as the body-weight is taken on

to the heels. The exercise can be repeated slowly about 6 times.

Exercise 4 (trunk) Crab

1. Many athletes struggle with this exercise but women and children tend to be more successful at it than men. The starting position is lying on the floor, hands behind the head and flat of the feet in a comfortable position under the knees.

2. The objective is to get the back into a high arch. The position should be held for 2 seconds, then the body should be lowered slowly.

Exercise 5 (arms) Trunk bend/hands clap

1. The athletes spread their legs shoulder-width apart, bend the trunk and spread their arms wide.

2. In a rhythmic fashion they sweep their arms down to clap hands just below the head, with their arms still extended.

3. The arms are then swept upwards and backwards while the trunk is bent and the head faces downwards.

4. Finally, the hands are clapped behind the back before sweeping down to be clapped near the floor again. A smooth action is maintained while the exercise is repeated about 6 times.

Exercise 6 (legs and spine) Hurdle

1. In a sitting position, one heel touches the buttock while the other leg stretches forwards with a 90° angle between the legs. Where possible, the body is upright.

2. In a slow, sustained fashion, the arms are stretched forward so that the fingers touch the toes and the head touches the knee. The exercise is repeated with the other foot in front. A total of about 6 attempts is ample.

Exercise 7 (all body) Power jump

After the slow jogging and gentle stretching, about 6 powerful jumps into the air, with an attempt to make the knees touch the chest, are useful before the training session begins.

Exercise 8 (lungs and skill) Accelerating runs

Before training or competition runs, in addition to stretching exercises athletes should run distances of about 50m three or four times, gradually increasing the speed. As well as the general stretching exercises, specific practices should be carried out, i.e. sprinters should run out of starting blocks two or three times, hurdlers should run over hurdles, relay runners should practise baton passing and receiving. After these preliminaries, a period of approximately ten minutes (dependent upon the climate) should be left before the race for the athlete to lie down in a warm, comfortable spot, close his eyes and 'gather' himself psychologically in preparation for the imminent competition.

SPRINTING (100, 200 & 400 METRES)

'Sprinters are born and not made.'

Anonymous

It can now be revealed that the above quotation was uttered by an international sprinter who hated training. He hoped that if it were to be repeated often enough, his coach would get to hear of it and would require less training from his athletes!

The truth is that sprinting is a skilful activity just like gymnastic somersaulting or football kicking. Such activities must be practised constantly to retain or improve an athlete's level of ability.

In addition there must also be a lot of activity outside the realm of running; circuit training, weight training, harness work, cross-country, *paarlauf* (pair-running) and hard sprint running.

The athlete

No particular body type can be described as the ideal for a sprinter. World record holders have included the small, wiry Mike Agostini, the heavy, powerful Bob Hayes and the tall, lithe Carl Lewis. One or two generalisations can be made about sprinters, however:

■ they tend to be powerful, have long stride length and fast leg action

■ some of them should try other events!

Too many athletes have been introduced only to the simple events – schools and clubs seldom attempt events which might well be more appropriate for them and their members. Many present-day 'sprinters' would achieve greater success in hurdles, triple jump, or even middle distances. One successful sprinter in Great Britain, Don Anthony, changed his event successfully in the 1950s to become an Olympic hammer thrower!

Equipment

● Competition clothing consists of vest (which *must* be worn), shorts, underwear or support, and track shoes (socks are also worn by some athletes, though tight socks should be avoided). The track shoes should be light (why carry extra weight?), and may be purchased so that the metal spikes can be replaced when worn, or for substituting indoor spikes. Spiked shoes are not difficult to get used to, and they improve everyone's performance. The expense for schoolchildren can be overcome if their physical education teacher organises an annual second-hand track shoe sale, so that little-worn shoes which are too small can be passed down to younger athletes.

● For training and warming-up purposes, a warm track suit, old sweater, and training shoes are also essential. The training shoes should be waterproof so that during winter training or the warm-up prior to a race, the feet are kept dry for as long as possible.

● Starting blocks are not essential for schoolchildren. In fact, some track meeting organisers will not permit some age groups to use them because of the time taken to fix them to the track. It is probably not in the interests of boys and girls of fifteen or less to use them because most athletes of this age start faster

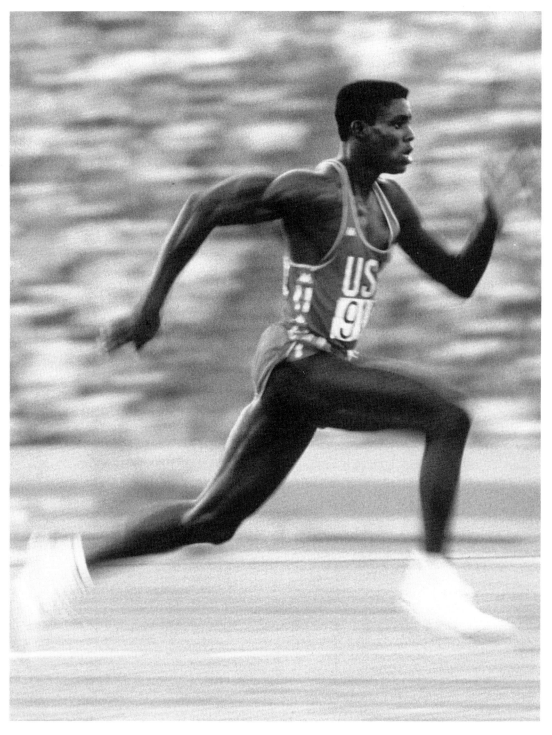

Carl Lewis (USA) demonstrates the essential elements of top-class sprinting – vigorous arm action and high knee lift

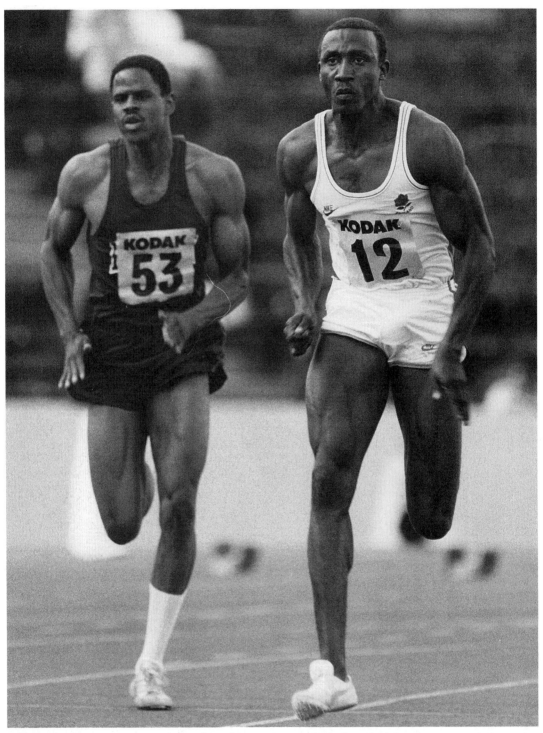

Modern day sprinters use heavy weights as part of their training, and this shows in their powerful musculature

tied to it and a second athlete holds the ropes. The objective is for the athlete in harness to run [25]m using the arms and legs vigorously, while [   ] behind gently pulls back on the harness. [   ] the 25m point, the one holding the rope [   ] the harness while the other pulls back on [   ] the return run.

Furthermore, sprinters should practise alongside other sprinters. Too many athletes train alone – gold medals are won only when opposition is beaten.

5. Bend running

There are many sprinters who are able to run 100 metres very well, but who fail to achieve equal success in the 200 metres. This is not

Blocks should be placed on the bend so that they are pointing towards the line and not down the middle of the lane

Harness running

23

(a) and (b) In both these photographs the athletes are demonstrating good, fast, relaxed running around the bend. Note the tendency to lean inwards – this is automatic and should not be overstressed by coaches

(b)

always due to their being unable to run longer distances, but often is because they do not modify their start on the bend, and do not run well around the bends because of lack of practice. To improve bend running ability, athletes have to practise bend running! Weekly schedules should incorporate half and full-bend runs at flat-out speed. Additionally, the setting of blocks needs attention. Whereas in the 100 metres race an athlete points his blocks down the middle of his lane, in the 200 (and 400) metres the blocks are set so that he will run out at a tangent to the bend, his first few strides taking him close to (but not touching) the inner edge of the lane.

6. Distribution of energy

In the 100 metres race there is insufficient time for less experienced athletes to think about anything else but running as fast as they can for the whole distance. Many would benefit from having their style 'tidied up' so that the head rolling from side to side and the body twisting were eliminated. Teachers or coaches could also ensure that the athletes adopted a more beneficial style if they were to insist on a more vigorous arm action, accompanied by a strong knee lift.

Many 200 metre races are lost because of an inaccurate belief that energy should be conserved around the bend, and that the real race is down the straight. From the start of the 200 metres the athletes should aim to get away as quickly as possible. They will find that their speed is naturally slowed down by the bend, but the aim should be to slow down as little as possible. Nearing the end of the bend, they should consciously attempt to accelerate as fast as possible into the straight and maintain this speed by vigorous knee and arm action.

The 400 metres race involves tactics for the distribution of energy which vary considerably, being dependent not only upon the age and sex of the athletes, but also upon whether the athlete is a 400 metres runner who has progressed from 100 and 200 metres, or whether he is an occasional 800 metres runner. Varying advice has been written about the 'English' and 'American' styles of running the 400 metres, namely an even distribution of

effort as opposed to a very fast first 200m. The author's opinion (and experience) is that there is a considerable amount of 'thinking' time in a 400 metres race, and so athletes should be given a number of tasks to perform during the race, for example:

(a) consciously attempt a very fast first bend,
(b) concentrate on relaxing down the 'back straight',
(c) accelerate into the final bend,
(d) over-emphasise arm drive and knee lift down the finishing straight.

The time for the first 100, 200 or 300m of a 400 metres run is something that coaches and athletes will determine as a result of experience, and the athlete will get used to these times through practice in training sessions. The main problem is not so much the setting of these targets, but getting the athlete to adhere to them when he has the immense distractions of the race to contend with, such as natural fear, the lane draw, the known performances of the opposition, the crowd noise, the weather, etc.

7. Finishing

Athletes will see top-class performers 'dipping' at the finishing line. This is a difficult skill to master. Beginners should be taught to run well past the line before they decelerate.

Training

When a coach looks at his athletes, he will observe that no two are identical in looks. Similarly, their needs are different and their weaknesses are different, and thus different schedules are required for each athlete, though with a similar plan.

The author's preference is never to give athletes the same schedule for more than two or three weeks. Boredom can soon set in and the resultant lack of effort means that the training is not so beneficial. Another helpful hint is *not* to use stop-watches very often in training. First of all, coaches are not normally good

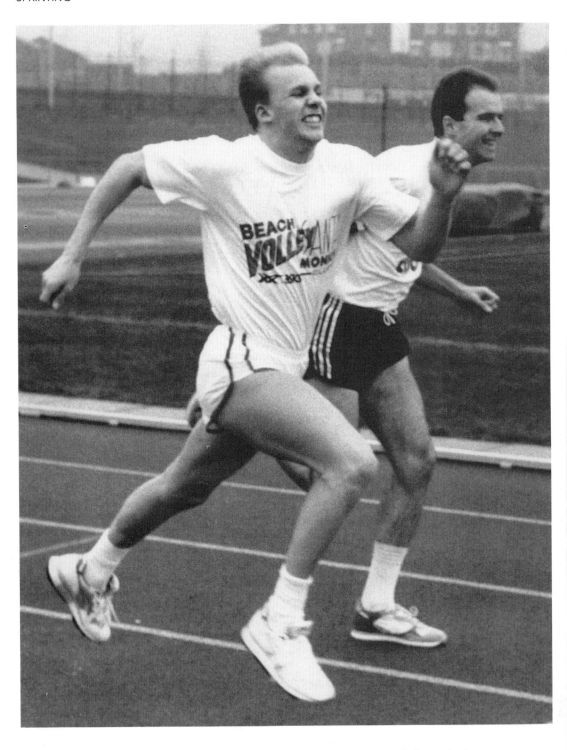

Gritting the teeth and clenching the fists when fatigue sets in does not increase speed. The emphasis should be on a greater arm drive and knee lift timekeepers; secondly, wind variations and the state of the track affect times; thirdly, times in training bear no relationship to competition performances; and fourthly, poor times in training can have a bad effect on athletes' morale.

   Usually, training is broken down into winter and summer schedules or off-season and during-season work. The following examples are taken from actual training programmes of good-class athletes and give an idea of the types of activity and where the emphases lie at different stages.

100 & 200 metres (men) (off-season)

DAY 1 ▶	Run 1 mile (1,600m) at a steady pace Do 20–30 minutes' circuit training
DAY 2 ▶	Sprint 50m, jog 50m; sprint 60m, jog 60m Sprint 70m, jog 70m; sprint 80m, jog 80m Sprint 90m, jog 90m; sprint 100m, jog 100m Rest for 10 minutes Reverse the previous procedure, that is Sprint 100m, jog 100m; sprint 90m, jog 90m Sprint 80m, jog 80m; sprint 70m, jog 70m Sprint 60m, jog 60m; sprint 50m, jog 50m
DAY 3 ▶	Rest day
DAY 4 ▶	Weight training
DAY 5 ▶	Sprint 60m from blocks five times, walking back to the start each time Rest for 5 minutes Sprint 60m five times as before Rest for 5 minutes Sprint 60m five times as before
DAY 6 ▶	'Free choice' session. Athlete can choose extra weight training session, or track session, or cross-country run, etc.
DAY 7 ▶	Rest day

100 & 200 metres (men)   (during season)

DAY 1 ▶	Jog 1 mile (1,600m) Do stretching exercises
DAY 2 ▶	Jog to a line, sprint 80m, walk back to start Repeat five times, attempting to accelerate during the last 20m of each run Rest for 10 minutes Sprint 80m six times as before
DAY 3 ▶	From a standing start, sprint 40m, walk 40m sprint 50m, walk 50m sprint 60m, walk 60m sprint 70m, walk 70m sprint 80m, walk 80m sprint 90m, walk 90m Rest for 10 minutes Reverse previous procedure, that is From a standing start, sprint 90m, walk 90m sprint 80m, walk 80m sprint 70m, walk 70m sprint 60m, walk 60m sprint 50m, walk 50m sprint 40m, walk 40m
DAY 4 ▶	Using starting blocks, sprint 50m five times Rest for 5 minutes sprint 50m five times as before Rest for 5 minutes sprint 50m five times as before
DAY 5 ▶	On grass, concentrating on relaxation, Sprint 120m, walk 120m, sprint 60m, walk 60m Repeat sequence twice Rest for 10 minutes Sprint 120m, walk 120m, sprint 60m, walk 60m Repeat sequence twice (If the DAY 7 competition is a tough one this day could simply consist of the DAY 1 schedule)
DAY 6 ▶	Rest day
DAY 7 ▶	Competition

100 & 200 metres (women)   (off-season)

DAY 1 ▶	Jog 800m Do 15–20 minutes' circuit training
DAY 2 ▶	Sprint 40m, jog 40m; sprint 50m, jog 50m Sprint 60m, jog 60m; sprint 70m, jog 70m Sprint 80m, jog 80m; 10 minutes' rest Reverse the previous procedure, that is Sprint 80m, jog 80m; sprint 70m, jog 70m Sprint 60m, jog 60m; sprint 50m, jog 50m Sprint 40m, jog 40m
DAY 3 ▶	Rest day
DAY 4 ▶	Weight training
DAY 5 ▶	Sprint 50m from blocks five times, walking back to the start each time Rest for 5 minutes Sprint 50m five times as before
DAY 6 ▶	'Free choice' session. Athlete can choose extra weight training session, or cross-country run, or game of squash, etc.
DAY 7 ▶	Rest day

100 & 200 metres (women)   (during season)

DAY 1 ▶	Jog 800m Do stretching exercises
DAY 2 ▶	Jog to a line, sprint 60m, walk back to start Repeat five times, attempting to accelerate towards the end of each run Rest for 10 minutes Sprint 60m six times as before

DAY 3 ▶	From a standing start, sprint 40m, walk 40m
	        sprint 50m, walk 50m
	        sprint 60m, walk 60m
	        sprint 70m, walk 70m
	        sprint 80m, walk 80m
	
	Rest for 10 minutes
	Reverse previous procedure, that is
	From a standing start, sprint 80m, walk 80m
	        sprint 70m, walk 70m
	        sprint 60m, walk 60m
	        sprint 50m, walk 50m
	        sprint 40m, walk 40m

continued over

DAY 4 ▶	Using starting blocks, sprint 50m four times Rest for 5 minutes Sprint 50m four times as before Rest for 5 minutes Sprint 50m four times as before

DAY 5 ▶	On grass, concentrating on relaxation, Sprint 100m, walk 100m, sprint 50m, walk 50m Repeat sequence twice Rest for 10 minutes Sprint 100m, walk 100m, sprint 50m, walk 50m Repeat sequence twice (If the DAY 7 competition is a tough one this day could simply consist of the DAY 1 schedule)
DAY 6 ▶	Rest day
DAY 7 ▶	Competition

400 metres (men) (off-season)

DAY 1 ▶	Run 1 mile (1,600m) at a steady pace Do 20–30 minutes' circuit training
DAY 2 ▶	Sprint 150m, jog back to starting point Sprint 200m, jog back to starting point Sprint 250m, jog back to starting point Sprint 300m, jog back to starting point Rest for 10 minutes Reverse previous procedure, that is Sprint 300m, jog back to starting point Sprint 250m, jog back to starting point Sprint 200m, jog back to starting point Sprint 150m, jog back to starting point
DAY 3 ▶	Rest day
DAY 4 ▶	Weight training
DAY 5 ▶	Sprint 80m six times from blocks on a bend in the track, jogging back to the start each time Rest for 10 minutes Sprint 80m six times as before

continued over

DAY 6 ▶	'Fartlek' run, that is 3–4 miles (approx. 5,000m) of jogging, striding and sprinting over a cross-country course
DAY 7 ▶	Rest day

400 metres (men)   (during season)

DAY 1 ▶	Jog 1 mile (1,600m) Do stretching exercises only
DAY 2 ▶	Sprint 200m in under 28 seconds Repeat twice, walking back to the start each time Rest for 10 minutes Sprint 200m in under 27 seconds Repeat twice, walking back to the start each time Rest for 10 minutes Sprint 200m in under 26 seconds Repeat twice, walking back to the start each time
DAY 3 ▶	Sprint 80m, walk back; sprint 150m, walk back Repeat sequence twice Rest for 10 minutes Sprint 80m, walk back; sprint 150m; walk back Repeat sequence twice
DAY 4 ▶	Run six times from blocks on the bend over a distance of 80m Rest for 10 minutes Run 80m six times as before
DAY 5 ▶	Run 100m six times, with the emphasis on relaxed running
DAY 6 ▶	Rest day
DAY 7 ▶	Competition

400 metres (women)   (off-season)

DAY 1 ▶	Run 1 mile (1,600m) at a steady pace Do 15–20 minutes' circuit training
DAY 2 ▶	Sprint 200m, jog 200m Sprint 200m, jog 200m Rest for 5 minutes Sprint 150m, jog 150m Sprint 150m, jog 150m Rest for 5 minutes Sprint 100m, jog 100m Sprint 100m, jog 100m
DAY 3 ▶	Rest day
DAY 4 ▶	Weight training
DAY 5 ▶	Sprint 60m six times from blocks on a bend in the track, jogging back to the start each time Rest for 10 minutes Sprint 60m six times as before
DAY 6 ▶	'Fartlek' run, that is 2–3 miles (approx. 4,000m) of jogging, striding and sprinting over a cross-country course
DAY 7 ▶	Rest day

400 metres (women)   (during season)

DAY 1 ▶	Jog 1 mile (1,600m) Do stretching exercises only
DAY 2 ▶	Sprint 100m, walk back Sprint 120m, walk back Sprint 140m, walk back Sprint 160m, walk back Rest for 10 minutes Sprint 160m, walk back Sprint 140m, walk back Sprint 120m, walk back Sprint 100m, walk back
DAY 3 ▶	Sprint 100m, walk back; sprint 50m, walk back Repeat sequence twice Rest for 10 minutes Sprint 100m, walk back; sprint 50m; walk back Repeat sequence twice

continued over

DAY 4 ▶ Sprint five times from blocks set on the bend over a distance of 60m, walking back each time
Rest for 10 minutes
Sprint 60m five times as before

DAY 5 ▶ Sprint 100m five times, with the emphasis on relaxed running

DAY 6 ▶ Rest day

DAY 7 ▶ Competition

Rules

There are a number of rules about sprint races of which even athletes and coaches are often ignorant. The following list of rules, though not complete, includes all the major international competition sprinting rules.

(a) Numbers shall be worn on the chest and the back in sprint races.
(b) Blocks may be used in sprint races, but must be approved by the Starter.
(c) The commands prior to the start of a race are: 'on your marks' and 'set' (in the language of the country in which the competition is held), followed by the pistol.
(d) If an athlete lifts a hand or foot from the ground before the pistol is fired, it is a false start.
(e) If an athlete is responsible for two false starts he is disqualified.
(f) During a race, athletes must remain in their own lanes.
(g) The winner is the athlete whose torso (excluding head, arms and legs) is first to be perpendicularly over the finishing line.

RELAYS

Shuttle relays

Where 400 metre tracks are not available, much enjoyment, effort and skill may be forthcoming from shuttle relays. These can be organised in the gymnasium or on playing fields and are not confined to one team per lane necessarily, because they could be run without the use of lanes; neither are they restricted to only four athletes per team.

Shuttle relay organisation consists of lining up the teams side by side, one half of each team behind a line facing the other half of each team some distance away, as illustrated below. On the signal from the teacher or coach, No. 1 runs to touch the outstretched hand of No. 2, who must not commence until No. 1 has crossed the predetermined line. No. 2 then runs to touch No. 3, and so on. If a baton is used, it reduces the tendency to cheat and introduces an additional skill.

Such relays could be introduced as warm-up activities at clubs and schools and could include mixed teams of men and women specialising in such different events as shot-put, high-jump, hurdles, etc.

Fig 1   Shuttle relays

(a) and (b) Relay practice – the shuttle relay

(b)

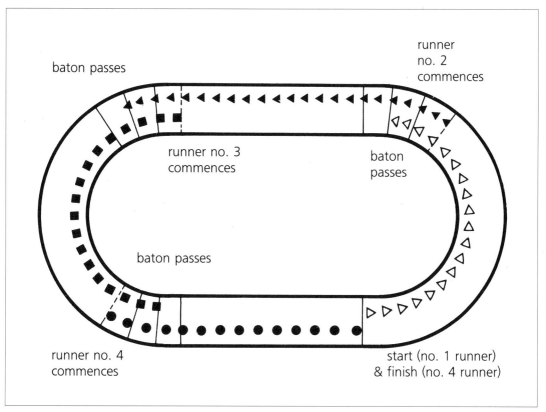

baton passes

runner
no. 2
commences

runner no. 3
commences

baton
passes

baton passes

runner no. 4
commences

start (no. 1 runner)
& finish (no. 4 runner)

Fig 2   4 × 100m relay

4 × 100 metres relay

Throughout the world there is a mistaken belief that all that is required to create a successful relay team is to put together the first four athletes from a school, club, or country's 100 metres championships and spend a small amount of time on baton practice. Some team selectors make a gesture to signify their greater understanding by including one or two 200 metres runners. But generally not enough time is spent considering what the needs are for each particular leg of the relay. The diagram above outlines the different characteristics of each leg, and on page 43 there are details of the needs of each runner.

Left **In this relay the superior technical training of the East Germans results in their being ahead of the team from the United States**

Baton passing

Primary school method

A simple method of passing the baton is the one illustrated below. The outgoing runner presents a target with his left arm into which the incoming runner places the baton. On receiving the baton, the outgoing runner changes it to his right hand, then continues running to present the baton in a similar fashion to the next runner.

Using this method, the outgoing runners simply stand inside the relay box and start jogging with the head turned to be able to see that the incoming runner does not stop through fatigue. A check mark should be placed on the track a 'safe' distance before the box, dependent upon the ages and speed of the athletes. When the incoming runner reaches the check mark, the outgoing runner sets off. The emphasis in this style is on receiving the baton with little risk of disqualification.

High school method

Older athletes who have had some experience of baton work may progress to a faster style of baton pass. In this method, the check marks are placed farther away from the outgoing runner. When the incoming runner reaches the check mark the outgoing runner runs away as fast as possible, not looking back, and extends his left hand back to await an upsweep pass from the incoming runner's right hand.

The baton is then changed to the right hand ready to pass to the left hand of the next runner. With this method the stretching back of the hand means that the incoming runner does not have to go as near to the outgoing runner, and so a faster relay results.

Downward sweep pass

Well-constructed relay teams can graduate to a method in which there is a higher risk of disqualification, but which gives a much faster overall speed of the baton. In the downward

(a) and (b) The primary school method of baton passing   **(b)**

Close-up of the hand action in the high school method

The high school method makes faster baton passing possible because the outgoing runner does not have to look back

sweep method the first runner holds the baton in the **right** hand, the second runner starts to the right of the lane and when runner No. 1 reaches a predetermined check mark, No. 2 runs off as fast as possible. At the seventh stride he puts back his left hand, palm uppermost, and No. 1 sweeps the baton down firmly into his left palm. No. 2 keeps the baton in his left hand and passes downwards to the **right** hand of No. 3, who runs around the bend and passes downwards to the **left** hand of No. 4. By not changing hands there is a considerable saving of time, and a faster overall time is normally recorded.

Upward sweep pass

The downward sweep technique of not changing the baton from one hand to the other can be employed using an upsweep. However, the athletes must make sure that they give

plenty of baton to the outgoing runner, otherwise time could be wasted having to adjust the baton in the hand.

Visual technique

This method is often used in 4 × 400 metre relays where the athletes are tiring towards the end of the race, and sometimes in 4 × 100 where children or unreliable athletes are used.

Progressive stages

1. Whatever method is employed, athletes must first be introduced to it by working in twos at walking pace. The athlete at the back places the

The downward sweep pass

The upward sweep pass

The visual technique for baton passing

Practising baton passing at speed

baton in the desired fashion into the hand of the athlete in the front, then walks briskly to the front to receive the baton from his partner. This continuous passing has the added objective of giving practice at receiving in both hands.

2. The next stage is to complete the passing routine at a jog. Here the additional difficulties of keeping the receiving arm still while jogging and of handing over the baton to a possibly moving target are introduced.

3. The speed of the exchange practice can be increased with all athletes having practice of receiving and passing the baton using alternately left and right hands. These practices enable athletes to discover whether they are better at receiving or passing a baton, and which of their hands is the most adept at this skill.

4. As soon as the baton passing has been practised at speed, it must be remembered that the baton must also be received within a limited area – the 'take-over zone' of 20 metres. To ensure that this is carried out accurately, check marks need to be used. These are marks placed on the track (on cinder tracks, a scratch mark made by the athlete's spiked shoes; on all-weather surfaces, a chalk mark or a strip of adhesive tape); when the mark is reached by the incoming runner, the outgoing runner knows that he must start running.

5. Check mark distances are calculated after much trial and error. The most convenient and accurate method of measuring them is for the outgoing runner to measure in foot lengths from the beginning of the take-over zone towards the athlete who is going to pass to him.

Calculating check marks for relay

The check mark of these athletes should be extended to save time in the passing of the baton

The athlete will be given a number of foot lengths to try by his teacher or coach. If, for instance, it is decided to use fifteen foot lengths as a check mark, a baton pass will be attempted at full speed using that distance check mark. If the incoming runner passes or comes too close to the outgoing runner, then the check mark needs to be extended to perhaps twenty foot lengths, and another attempt made. If on this occasion the incoming runner does not catch the outgoing runner, then the check mark is reduced to, say, eighteen foot lengths and so on, until the baton pass is successfully carried out.

The check mark of these athletes is too far away, hence the unsuccessful attempt to pass the baton before the end of the relay box

Training

Baton passing must be practised frequently and at full speed. It is no use the incoming runner running in slowly and then accelerating over a short distance; this creates inconsistency because during a race the incoming runner will have run over 100m by the time he reaches the take-over zone. Training runs should require the incoming runner to run at least 50–60 metres.

Additionally, there must be consistency in the speed at which the outgoing runner starts his run, and so his starting position should be as near to a sprint race 'set' position as possible

This athlete places one hand on the floor for support as he awaits the incoming runner

This athlete's fingers are not strong enough to support her in the 'set' position but she does adopt a crouched stance

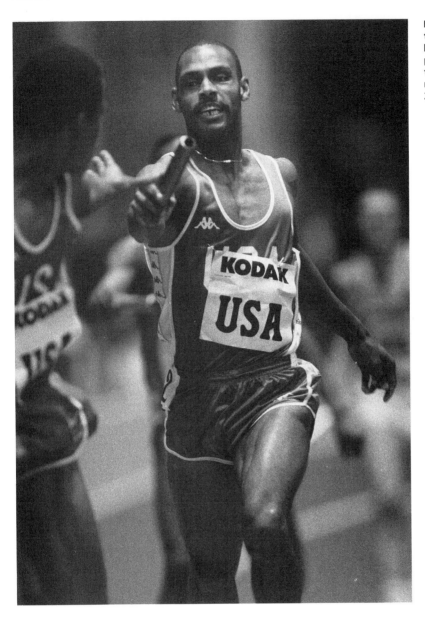

In this 4 × 400m race a tired incoming runner hands over with a visual pass to his outgoing team-mate. The baton must be passed in the 20-metre zone

(see the two examples at the foot of page 41). Adult athletes will probably place one hand on the floor for support; those who do not have strong fingers will not be able to hold that position, but will nevertheless adopt a 'crouch' stance. They will stand to one side of the lane, that is if they are to receive the baton in the left hand, they will stand to the right of their lane.

Their bodies will point forwards, only the heads being turned to look at the check mark.

Practices should take place at different parts of the track, so that some baton passing occurs on the bend of the track, some on the straight. Finally, once a team has been selected, they need to practise over the full distance with opposition.

Runner number	Distance he runs	Distance he carries the baton	Special skills necessary
1	100 metres	100 metres	Must be a good starter Must be able to run around a bend
2	120 metres	100 metres	Must be able to receive baton in left hand Must be a good 'straight' runner
3	120 metres	100 metres	Must be able to receive baton in right hand Must be a good 'bend' runner
4	120 metres	100 metres	Must be able to receive baton in left hand Must be a good 'straight' runner Must not give in under pressure

The details given refer to an ideal situation in which the baton is received half-way through the relay box at all exchanges. Even so, it will be noticed that no two 'legs' are alike in the distance run and in the responsibility of the runner, and selecting a 4 × 100m relay team therefore requires a great deal of thought before the practising begins.

Rules

(a) In 4 × 100 and 4 × 400 metre relays, there must be four runners who run the distance specified. (Substitutes are permitted in semi-finals or finals).

(b) The baton must be passed and not thrown from one athlete to the other.

(c) The baton must be passed within the 20 metre take-over zone.

(d) If the baton is dropped, the athlete who drops it must pick it up, and in doing so must not impede other athletes in the race.

(e) The usual rules relating to sprinting apply, namely use of starting blocks, starter's commands, the necessity of athletes staying in their own lanes, the judging and timing of athletes.

(f) Contravention of the rules leads to the whole team being disqualified.

HURDLES

Hurdling can be an event in which athletes run as fast as possible between the hurdles and leap over the barriers in a variety of ungainly styles. There are a number of reasons why inexpert hurdling is carried out in this fashion:

- lack of knowledge of hurdling technique
- lack of mobility in the hip joint and spine
- fear of the obstacles.

At top level athletics these factors must be overcome. However, at school level hurdling can still be an enjoyable, unusual challenge to those children who will never be able to become good hurdlers.

The athlete

Hurdlers must essentially be tall, long-legged, fast, supple, powerful athletes. There have of course been exceptions, such as the Great Britain Olympic 400 metres hurdler Peter Warden, who was only about 5ft 6in tall (1.65m), and the Australian woman Olympic medallist Pamela Ryan. But such small athletes need to work harder to overcome their height disadvantage.

In the past, Olympic hurdlers have included athletes such as Vic Matthews of Great Britain, who was relatively slow over the 100 metres sprint race, but whose exceptional ability over the hurdles compensated for his lack of speed. Recently, however, top-class hurdlers such as Colin Jackson (Great Britain) have also been among the best sprinters in the country.

Equipment

No personal equipment is needed additional to that of a sprinter. But as men and women of different ages race over different heights of hurdles with different distances between, it is essential to know these to ensure that athletes are training for the correct event.

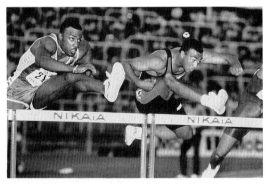

On the right of the picture Colin Jackson (Great Britain) demonstrates an excellent low position over the hurdle

The static hurdling position is useful in helping to establish faults, for example in this photograph we can see that the athlete in the centre is very stiff. The position does not improve hurdling performance

Girls and women	Race distance	Hurdle height	No. of hurdles	Distance from start to 1st hurdle	Distance between hurdles	Distance from last hurdle to Finish
Age						
13 & 14	75m	76cm	8	11.5m	7.5m	11m
15 & 16	80m	76cm	8	12m	8m	12m
17 & 18	100m	84cm	10	13m	8.5m	10.5m
19	200m	76cm	10	16m	19m	13m
	400m	76m	10	45m	35m	40m
Also for						
17 & 18	400m	76cm	10	45m	35m	40m
19+	400m	76cm	10	45m	35m	40m
Boys and men						
Age						
13 & 14	80m	84cm	8	12m	8m	12m
15 & 16	100m	91.5cm	10	13m	8.5m	10.5m
17 & 18	110m	99cm	10	13.72m	9.14m	14.02m
19	110m	106.7cm	10	13.72m	9.14m	14.02m
Also for						
17 & 18	400m	84cm	10	45m	35m	40m
19+	400m	91.4cm	10	45m	35m	40m

The hurdle must be weighted so that it takes a force of 3kg to overturn them in races for 16-year-olds and under, and 4kg for 17-year-olds and above. The weights may be separate from the hurdle or built in.

Progressive stages

Teachers and coaches often fail to realise what hurdling really is. They tend to set out one or two hurdles and require children or athletes to get over them, regardless of the fact that even to adults the hurdle can appear to be a terrifying obstacle. Other teachers and coaches tend to overemphasise the 'hurdling position', or what the coach assumes the athlete's pose should be when he is going over the hurdle. Thus the athlete is required to practise this position while sitting on the ground or while walking around.

It would be better if hurdling were to be regarded as a race in which an athlete sprinted

The older type of hurdle (left) has weights supplied separately from the rest of the hurdle. These are screwed on to the appropriate spot on the hurdle leg depending on the hurdle race it is being used for. The modern type of hurdle (right) has the weights built into the leg. These can be moved forwards and backwards to ensure the correct 'toppling' force

This is a very useful flexibility exercise, but it should not replace actual hurdles practice

one lane the 'obstacles' will be close together, then adjacent lanes will contain a gradually increasing distance between the 'obstacles', as shown below.

The objective is for all the athletes to start in the lane with 5m gaps and attempt to run over the lines in a regular pattern of running with the same foot stepping over the line each time. By moving up to the 6m or 7m lanes, the long-legged athletes will finally find a lane that suits them, and the group will be divided among the lanes according to their leg-length, stride-length, or athletic ability. Gradually they must increase their speed, at which time they might find the need to move up to the next lane.

as fast as he could from A to B whilst clearing hurdles en route. Then from the beginning the emphasis would be on speed over a distance, and not artificial poses or the clearing of one hurdle.

1. Beginners should be confronted with a number of different lanes in which strips of wood, chalk marks or some other indications present 'obstacles' to the athletes' progress. In

2. When the teacher or coach is convinced that all the athletes are working satisfactorily, the next stage may be introduced. Using bamboo canes or similar pieces of wood placed across bricks, skittles, small waste paper bins or similar objects that are about 20–30cm high, the same practice can continue, except that this time the obstacles are slightly higher. The emphasis will again be on covering the distance as fast as possible with the same foot stepping over the obstacle each time. Some athletes will start to

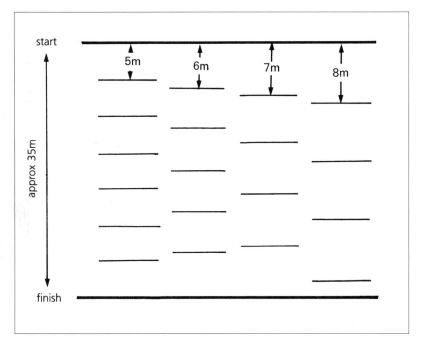

Fig 3   An exercise designed to help the athletes discover their stride length

Hurdles practice over bamboo canes

The hurdling action is the sprinter's high knee lift action

knock the wood off its supports, in which case they need to go back to the next lane down. After more practice with the teacher or coach emphasising good sprinting technique, another stage will be necessary.

3. In the next stage, the teacher or coach simply raises the height of the cane to approximately 40–50cm, and practice continues. Again, some might need to go back to another lane, and those who are not lifting their knees high in the normal sprinting position will be knocking the cane from the support. However, there should still be no jumping over the obstacle.

Should the athletes be young or small there might be a need to go on to the next stage soon – that is if the majority are now beginning to knock the cane down while adopting a normal sprinting action.

4. The first thing to do at this stage is to show the children or athletes the safe and the dangerous aspects of hurdling. It will be pointed out that the hurdle must always be encountered from the front, that is where the two bases of the hurdle are pointing. If the hurdle is

The rear leg comes through with the knee and toe pointing outwards

The athlete going in the wrong direction will get hurt if he hits the hurdle

The athlete going in the correct direction will simply knock the hurdle down if she hits it

accidentally touched while hurdling in this direction, it will simply fall to the floor, whereas if the athlete hits a hurdle because he has been foolish enough to go over it in the wrong direction, then the hurdle will be raised higher from the ground and the athlete could be hurt.

Next it is demonstrated how the first part of the sprinting action, a vigorous raising of the front knee, can apply over the hurdle. The rear knee, however, cannot come through high otherwise it would hit the hurdle, so it has to point outwards. Similarly the rear toe cannot point down, so it too points outwards.

This demonstration can take the form of the teacher or coach stepping over the hurdle slowly for all to see and the athletes doing likewise. But at this time it must also be pointed out that if athletes go over hurdles with the body upright, then their centres of gravity cover too great a distance and they will therefore take a longer time to complete the race.

The athletes should practise going over one hurdle to begin with at its lowest height (this is usually 76cm, but sometimes 60cm or 68cm), remembering the rear leg action and attempting to keep the body low.

5. After the initial practice over one hurdle, the athletes can be asked to look at their friends so that they can appreciate the good and bad points of technique. At the early stage they will tend to jump because of fear of hitting the hurdle with their knees or feet. With the growth of confidence they will go over at a lower

Teachers will have to allow beginners to 'get the feel' of the movement before they attempt to go over at full speed

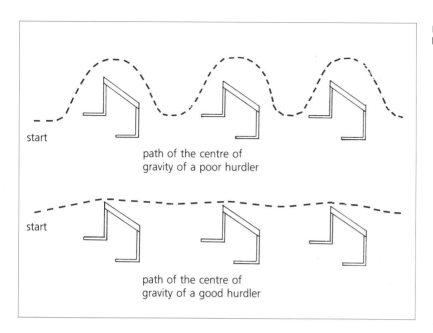

Fig 4 Good and bad hurdling technique

start

path of the centre of gravity of a poor hurdler

start

path of the centre of gravity of a good hurdler

height, and can then be coached further. At this stage, however, some will obviously stand out as non-hurdlers. Teachers or coaches should consider the advisability of keeping such athletes on the previous practices of 'hurdling' over canes, rather than continue to force them to jump over an obstacle which they find frightening.

6. Further coaching points include:
- attempting to touch the leading toes with the opposite hand
- attempting to touch the leading knee with the chin
- attempting to lay the chest along the leading thigh.

7. The next stage will be to introduce a second hurdle so that not only does the athlete clear one hurdle, but he now has to think about a pattern of three strides between this and the next hurdle (see the diagram on page 50).

8. Within a short period of time, yet further hurdles must be introduced because otherwise athletes can be preoccupied with hurdle clearance instead of with getting from start to finish as fast as possible.

9. Practice must then be given from a starting line to the first hurdle because of the difficulty encountered by some who might have to change their feet around at the start. This might be necessary in order to accommodate a pattern

An athlete practising the hand to opposite toe, knee touching chin, chest along thigh position

Fig 5 Working out the stride pattern for the hurdles

of strides that will lead the athlete to the first hurdle with the correct leg in front. After this point it is simply more practice at hurdling, more sprinting, more suppling of the hips and spine and more strength work which are required.

Different distances – different considerations

Though a number of world-class hurdlers are equally effective over both 110 metres and 400 metres (e.g. Alan Pascoe and David Hemery), the majority of hurdlers are normally either short *or* long hurdles race specialists. Teachers and coaches should therefore be aware of the different essentials required in the various hurdles races.

In this photograph we see the athletes attacking the hurdles, which is preferable to floating over the barriers

Short hurdle events

These require precision at the start of a race. Normally about eight strides are taken to the first hurdle, though some tall athletes manage to complete the distance in seven strides. There must be much practice with starting block spacings and different feet in front at the start to achieve the ideal pattern of strides to the first hurdle. This part of the race needs fast, vigorous arm and leg action.

The athlete should 'attack' the first hurdle, driving towards it with a vigorous body dip and pulling the rear leg through quickly. In the senior events, an athlete will normally take off about 2m before the hurdle and land 1·2m the other side of it. Thus with a vigorous arm action and stride length of over 2m, he can cover the distance between the hurdles adequately. When they complete the last hurdle, athletes are slowing down and tend to think that the race is over. They should go vigorously for the finishing line with arms and knees and not simply dive the last few metres with chins forward and arms flying behind them.

Long hurdle events

These require the ability of the athlete to run longer than the hurdle distance at fast pace. A guide is the fact that good hurdlers run the 400 metres hurdles only 3–4 seconds slower than they run the 400 metres flat race.

In the approach to the first hurdle, an athlete should practise a consistent pattern of strides, to which he will always keep in training and competition.

As the longer races have lower hurdles than the 110 metres race, the amount of body-dip is

At the end of a hurdles race there tends to be a loss of form. Athletes should train to *run* past the line and not *dive* for it

less and the emphasis is not so much on a vigorous movement as on a fast clearance.

Between hurdles an odd number of strides is usual, but world-class performers practise clearances with both legs so that when fatigue sets in they can change their pattern of strides if necessary.

The run-in from the last hurdle is very important in the longer races because of the greater distance there is to the finishing line. The athlete should try not to 'tighten up' and should attempt to maintain the rhythm used between the hurdles.

Training

Hurdlers could fool many a bystander into believing that they were training hard by simply going over the hurdles often (but slowly), by laboriously repeating the 'hurdle position' on the floor, by 'high-stepping' over hurdles and by employing high-kicks and other hip mobility exercises. The better performers, however, work hard in training and do not play around with useless, unrelated skills. Because of the range of abilities, differing age-groups, and different hurdle heights and distances, it is difficult to suggest an 'average' man's or woman's training

schedule, but what can be illustrated are the kinds of activity in which the athletes can be participating in winter and summer.

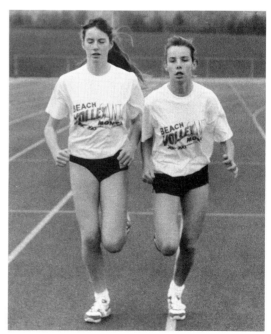

The athlete on the right in this photograph is liable for disqualification for impeding the other athlete's progress

Short hurdles race (men)
(off-season)

DAY 1 ▶ 30-minute Fartlek

DAY 2 ▶ 1 mile (1,600m) run and circuit training or weight training

DAY 3 ▶ Run 80m over hurdles six times
Run 100m with no hurdles six times

DAY 4 ▶ Weight training

DAY 5 ▶ Train hard on track with sprinters

DAY 6 ▶ Using a crouch start,
go fast over 1 hurdle (hurdling)
go fast over 2 hurdles (hurdling)
go fast over 3 hurdles (hurdling)
go fast over 4 hurdles (hurdling)
go fast over 5 hurdles (hurdling)
go fast over 6 hurdles (hurdling)

Rest
Using a crouch start,
go fast over 6 hurdles (hurdling)
go fast over 5 hurdles (hurdling)
go fast over 4 hurdles (hurdling)
go fast over 3 hurdles (hurdling)
go fast over 2 hurdles (hurdling)
go fast over 1 hurdle (hurdling)

DAY 7 ▶ Rest day

Short hurdles race (women)
(off-season)

DAY 1 ▶ 20-minute Fartlek

DAY 2 ▶ 1 mile (1,600m)
Do circuit training

DAY 3 ▶ Run 60m over hurdles five times
Run 80m without hurdles five times

DAY 4 ▶ Do weight training

DAY 5 ▶ Train with sprinters on track

DAY 6 ▶ Using a crouch start,
go fast over 1 hurdle (hurdling)

continued over

go fast over 2 hurdles (hurdling)
go fast over 3 hurdles (hurdling)
go fast over 4 hurdles (hurdling)
go fast over 5 hurdles (hurdling)

Rest for about 7 minutes
Using a crouch start,
go fast over 5 hurdles (hurdling)
go fast over 4 hurdles (hurdling)
go fast over 3 hurdles (hurdling)
go fast over 2 hurdles (hurdling)
go fast over 1 hurdle (hurdling)

DAY 7 ▶ Rest day

Short hurdles race (men)
(during season)

DAY 1 ▶ Jog, do stretching exercises and work on faults

DAY 2 ▶ Train hard with sprinters on track

DAY 3 ▶ Run over six hurdles six times
Run 50m six times

DAY 4 ▶ Train with sprinters from blocks over 60m; repeat five times
Run from blocks over six hurdles; repeat four times

DAY 5 ▶ Short sprint session

DAY 6 ▶ Rest day

DAY 7 ▶ Competition

Short hurdles race (women)
(during season)

DAY 1 ▶ Light day, working on technique faults

DAY 2 ▶ Train hard on track with sprinters

DAY 3 ▶ Run over five hurdles; repeat five times
Run 50m six times

DAY 4 ▶ Train with sprinters from blocks over 60m; repeat five times

continued over

	Run from blocks over six hurdles; repeat four times
DAY 5 ▶	Short sprint session
DAY 6 ▶	Rest day
DAY 7 ▶	Competition

Long hurdles race (men)
(off-season)

DAY 1 ▶	40-minute Fartlek
DAY 2 ▶	Weight training or circuit training
DAY 3 ▶	Run over five correctly-spaced hurdles; repeat four times, working on approach run and stride pattern Run 200m four times
DAY 4 ▶	Weight training
DAY 5 ▶	Train hard with 400m flat race men
DAY 6 ▶	Train with high hurdlers or run over five hurdles twice
DAY 7 ▶	Rest day

Long hurdles race (women)
(off-season)

DAY 1 ▶	30-minute Fartlek
DAY 2 ▶	Run 1,600m at steady pace 15–20 minutes' circuit training
DAY 3 ▶	Run over five correctly-spaced hurdles; repeat four times, working on approach run and stride pattern Run 200m four times
DAY 4 ▶	Weight training
DAY 5 ▶	Train hard with 400m flat race women

continued over

DAY 6 ▶ Train with high hurdlers
or run over five hurdles twice

DAY 7 ▶ Rest day

Long hurdles race (men)
(during season)

DAY 1 ▶ Jog, do stretching exercises, work on faults

DAY 2 ▶ Train hard with 400m flat race men

DAY 3 ▶ Run over five correctly-spaced hurdles; repeat
three times
Run 150m three times
Run 60m three times

DAY 4 ▶ Train from blocks around the first bend,
110m, six times
Run from blocks over five hurdles; repeat four
times

DAY 5 ▶ Short sprint session with 200m and 400m
athletes

DAY 6 ▶ Rest day

DAY 7 ▶ Competition

Long hurdles race (women)
(during season)

DAY 1 ▶ Jog, do stretching exercises, work on faults

DAY 2 ▶ Train hard with 400m flat race women

DAY 3 ▶ Run over five correctly-spaced hurdles; repeat
three times
Run 120m three times; run 50m three times

DAY 4 ▶ Train from blocks around the first bend,
110m, six times
Run from blocks over five hurdles; repeat four
times

continued over

DAY 5 ▶ Short sprint session with 100m and 200m athletes

DAY 6 ▶ Rest day

DAY 7 ▶ Competition

Rules

(a) Athletes must go **over** the hurdles (some tend to swing a leg around the side of a hurdle).
(b) If the hurdles are weighted, all can be knocked down; otherwise an athlete is disqualified if he knocks down three or more hurdles.

(c) Athletes must keep in their own lanes.
(d) The usual rules about start and finish in sprinting apply equally to hurdles races (see page 33).

MIDDLE DISTANCES AND CROSS-COUNTRY RUNNING

'The secret of running is not to get out of breath.'

Anonymous

To the layman, distance running must appear to be the least complicated form of track and field athletics. There is no aerodynamic equipment necessary as in the throwing events; no resorting to clandestine use of anabolic steroids in order to develop a grotesque, bulky body; no preoccupation with technique practice as in the jumps events. In fact, it might seem that all a distance runner needs to do to improve is simply run, run and run more.

In the past, middle-distance runners were often athletes who ran cross-country in the winter because they enjoyed running through different types of terrain. Some of them did not run track races in the summer because they found running laps around the track boring. Some used the track season to 'keep fit' in preparation for their cross-country racing season, whereas others were track athletes who used the cross-country season to 'keep fit' for the summer track season.

Sir Roger Bannister, Chris Chataway and Brian Hewson (all sub-four-minute mile runners) are examples of athletes who did not run competitively in the cross-country season. World track record holders Derek Ibbotson and Gordon Pirie, on the other hand, competed at international level in both cross-country and track events.

We can see, therefore, that middle-distance runners are selective in the type of running they do. Similarly, a study of the types of training, the diets and the involvement of physiologists with middle-distance runners would indicate that nowadays planning for improvement of the runners' abilities is more sophisiticated than many people imagine.

The athlete

World-class performers in middle and longer distance events have included a range of body types. There have been tall, slim athletes like Sir Roger Bannister and Kip Keino; diminutive, wiry athletes like Bruce Tulloh and Zola Budd; muscular athletes such as Mike Rawson, Vladimir Kuts and Jarmila Kratochvilova; and finally, a group of slightly disabled people, which includes asthmatics, and athletes with such deformities as a 'withered arm'.

The main fundamental to achieve success in running distances is the capacity to withstand hard work. This necessity for prolonged physical

In the last decade, 10,000m and various road races such as the marathon have been opened up to the female athletes. Here Liz McColgan (Great Britain), Greta Weitz (Norway) and Ingrid Christiansen (Sweden) take a rest from the pounding of hard roads to run on the relatively painless rubber track

activity makes it vital that teachers and coaches should satisfy themselves that medical advice has been obtained and confirms that the athletes are physically capable of withstanding sustained physiological stress.

Additionally, the precaution should be taken of having regular checks made to ensure that when the intensity of training increases, or when the schoolchild is developing, no excessive amounts of work are being imposed.

Sound hearts, however, cannot be 'strained'. In fact, training makes the heart more efficient; running makes the athlete healthier. Another attractive feature of running is that for the less skilful person who does not achieve success at jumping or throwing, or who is not of the body type to be able to participate in games, this is an enjoyable, challenging outlet.

Equipment

Though this may appear to be a superfluous section, there are a number of considerations for middle distance and cross-country runners.

● For track running, the athlete will eventually find a style of track shoe that suits him. A pair of shoes on which the spikes can be changed is recommended because of the many different types of surface that the athlete will be required to run on. With an all-weather track, shorter spikes will be required; on cinder tracks very long spikes will be used; on indoor tracks some

Steve Cram (Great Britain), a very tall, wiry athlete and short, stocky Pete Elliott (Great Britain) are both Olympic medallists, illustrating the fact that middle distance runners come in different shapes and sizes. The common factor is very low resting pulse rate

athletes prefer to run barefoot or use a light training shoe.

Cross-country shoes are available in a number of forms. The sole can be ribbed or rubber studded to provide grip on slippery surfaces, whereas on a cross-country course that is flat, hard grass and dry, an athlete might choose to wear spiked shoes. Whatever is selected should be comfortable, previously worn (new shoes might cause blisters) and not too heavy.

● Athletes tend to wear the same vest repeatedly, because it is their 'lucky' vest, or their club vest. But there should be other considerations. If it is a very hot day, a string vest with many holes in it would physiologically be preferable to a cotton or nylon vest. On a cold, wintry day, light long-sleeved vests or shirts might be more appropriate. Vests, shorts and track suits should be washed regularly to prevent skin irritations.

● Other useful items include a stop watch, ballet-tights and woollen hat for winter training, salt tablets for hot-weather climates in which athletes tend to suffer from cramp, and a diary of training – recording not only what was done, but how it felt (this assists a coach in future schedule planning).

After much trial and error athletes will find shoes that suit them

Name	Time	Time difference from previous runner	Time difference from last runner
Andrews	10min	0	1min 50sec
Bloggs	10min 25sec	25sec	1min 25sec
Carter	10min 40sec	15sec	1min 10sec
Davies	11min	20sec	50sec
Evans	11min 15sec	15sec	35sec
Frost	11min 50sec	35sec	0

Progressive stages

For the teacher or club coach who needs to build up schoolchildren or athletes gradually to a point at which they can be given individual schedules, it is useful to get them involved enjoyably with groups of other people of the same age or ability. To begin with, the athlete will wish to know how he compares with others, so a short race over a cross-country course would be a useful guide. Dependent upon the ages of the athletes, a distance of approximately 3,000m could be selected. (British rules require that boys and girls must be at least thirteen years of age before they compete in cross-country races. For that age group the maximum distances are 5,000m for boys, and 3,000m for girls.)

1. Initial races

The group set off all together from a point which ensures a sufficiently long distance to the first gate, gap in a hedge, or other funnelling that could result in a bunching-up of athletes. On reaching the finish, each athlete is timed to the nearest second, and a ranking list is prepared showing the name of the athlete, his time and by what amount of time he beat the next man. An additional column shows in reverse order by how many minutes and/or seconds the last man was behind each runner, as illustrated above.

For the next occasion, the same race can be held, but this time each athlete will be motivated to attempt to:

- win
- beat an athlete who beat him on the previous occasion
- beat his previous time
- narrow the time difference between himself and the runner ahead of him
- increase the distance between himself and the runner behind.

Such organisation creates interest and ensures that schoolchildren and athletes put in more effort.

2. Ringing the changes

Another form of running training that can be adopted is to take the final column of the race detailed above, and start a race with Frost setting off alone; his objective is not to be overtaken. 35 seconds later Evans sets off with the same objective and also attempts to overtake Frost. 50 seconds later Davies sets off and so on until, 1 min 50 secs after Frost started, Andrews leaves, hoping to beat his previous best time for the course and overtake as many athletes as possible en route.

The results of this race can show:

- who had the fastest time for the course
- which athletes beat their previous best time
- how many athletes overtook others during the race, etc.

Such changes of run lend interest, provide incentive for greater effort, and often increase the enjoyment. Further modes of training in the early stages can include pairing off the runners, e.g. Andrews and Frost (the best and poorest), Bloggs and Evans, Carter and Davies. The objective of such a race would be that the combined times of each pair would be recorded, and those obtaining the lowest time would win.

3. Hares and hounds and paper chase

Other popular forms of running have included in the past Hares and Hounds, where one or two athletes set off over a known course a minute or so before the remainder who attempt to catch him/them before he/they return(s) back to the starting place. In countries where the litter laws permit it, an interesting form of competition is for two runners to set off with bags of small pieces of paper (or sawdust, or chalk) on their backs. Their course is a secret, and they are given one or two minutes' start. The pursuers see the direction in which the athletes have gone, but once out of sight they can change direction provided they leave a trail of chalk, paper, etc., showing where they have gone. The objective is to catch the trail-leavers before they return back to the starting point.

Related to this type of activity is orienteering, a sport which involves participants with maps and compasses covering a predetermined route,

visiting a number of checkpoints, and attempting to complete the course as quickly as they can. For further details see *EP Sport Orienteering* (A&C Black, 1980).

4. Track practices

Having provided a base of fitness through increasing amounts of enjoyable running, the teacher or coach can begin to organise other practices based at the track. In the first instance, athletes can be required to carry out simple repetition runs similar to those outlined in the 'Sprinting' chapter of this book; then they can follow an introduction to the paarlauf (pair-running) system. Paarlauf is an interesting form of training or racing in which a racing distance, say eight laps of the track, is first decided upon. The athletes are divided into pairs and each pair decides how to divide the race between them; only one of the athletes needs to be running at any one time. There are a number of ways of doing it:

(i) athlete 'A' can run the first four laps and athlete 'B' the last four;
(ii) athlete 'A' can run the first two laps, then athlete 'B' two laps, then athlete 'A' two laps, concluding with athlete 'B' two laps;
(iii) they can run alternate laps;

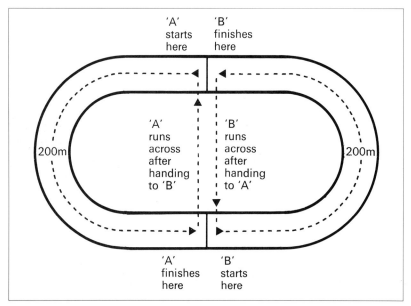

'A' starts here   'B' finishes here

'A' runs across after handing to 'B'   'B' runs across after handing to 'A'

200m   200m

'A' finishes here   'B' starts here

Fig 6   Track practice for middle distance running

Some athletes tend to adopt track running styles in cross-country races. Sometimes this is inappropriate and results in wasted expenditure of energy

(iv) athlete 'A' can run 200m and touch athlete 'B' (as in a relay), who runs the next 200m. In the meantime athlete 'A' cuts across the centre grass area of the track to his original starting point where athlete 'B' hands over the race to him. Athlete 'B' also cuts across the track ready to take over at his own 200m point.
(v) if 'A' is a better athlete than 'B' it may be decided to allocate over half of the running to 'A'.

Having begun to mix track work with cross-country practices, the teacher or coach will now be able to observe which athletes are ready to be given individual training programmes.

Training – theories

Style

Obviously an uneconomical running technique must be cured by the teacher or coach, but it is stressed that there is no ideal method of running. Emil Zatopek adopted a head and shoulder roll with tongue hanging out and an agonised facial expression; Kip Keino had a massive stride length and a most relaxed look about him; Zola Budd shuffled along in bare feet with arms bunched tightly across her body.

The important criterion is comfort. If an athlete's natural style is mechanically inefficient, causing him to expend extra energy, then the coach will modify the style; otherwise, there need be no interference. Breathing should be through the mouth and nose, there should be no attempt to lengthen the stride, and there should be a minimum of tension especially in the face and neck muscles.

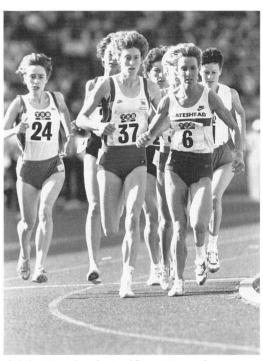

Christina Boxer is a short-striding patterer, whereas Kirsty Wade is a long-striding athlete, illustrating the fact that middle distance runners have a variety of styles

At the end of a race the emphasis should be on high knee lift and vigorous arm action. Sebastian Coe (Great Britain) demonstrates these two good qualities

Towards the end of a race (and, in the case of cross-country running, when running uphill), the style will necessarily change, the knees coming through higher and the arms driving more. In fact a sprinter's style will be adopted.

Long-distance as training

It is not only athletes of the distant past who have used the long-distance method for the bulk of their training. Peter Snell and Murray Halberg of New Zealand were both Olympic medallists trained by Arthur Lydiard, who claimed that all his runners were marathon runners. Thus although Snell won the gold medal in the 1960 Olympics in the 800 metres, Lydiard expected him to run marathon distances in training.

Some athletes who believe in the value of this system will train well over 100 miles in total each week, and will include runs of 20 miles or more on at least one day. Some athletes doing this kind of training are 800 metres runners! But athletes should not rely solely on this method, for though it has an advantageous effect on the circulorespiratory system and therefore provides a good basis for other types of training, actual racing consists of changes of pace including fast bursts as well as the slower pace, and so the heart needs to be accustomed to a variety of changes during training.

Interval training

Another group of athletes of yesteryear and the present day have preferred this systematic form of training, including Sebastian Coe, Steve Ovett, Vladimir Kuts, Emil Zatopek and Sir Roger Bannister. In interval training, the objective is to adapt the heart to the stress of running in endurance events. When training over distances in the region of 100, 200 and 400m, it has been found that middle-distance runners' hearts become stronger and pump blood around the muscles in greater volume, provided they run the chosen distance fast and take a pause of about 45–90 seconds before they run the next repetition.

German physiologists have shown that after a fast run of 200m the heart fills rapidly with blood. If the athlete jogs slowly for about 45 seconds, the amount of blood arriving at the heart is decreased. Should the athlete then repeat the procedure many times, with 'intervals' of sprinting followed by 'intervals' of slow jogging, the cavities of the heart increase in size and adapt themselves to receive more blood, thus providing more fresh blood to be supplied throughout the body. During a training session this system can gradually lose its effect. This has been shown to occur when an athlete's heart-rate is over 180 beats per minute.

Coaches therefore tend to limit their athletes' sprints to the period when the heart-rate is between 120 and 150 beats per minute, the rest between each run allowing the heart-rate to drop to that range.

Criticisms of the method include:

(a) it is boring
(b) it makes an athlete too dependent on stop-watch performance
(c) the volume of blood pumped out of the heart at each stroke is only one consideration, the number of strokes per minute also being important.

Tempo running

In addition to efficient hearts and lungs, athletes must also consider the fatigue in the arms, shoulders and leg muscles that is evident at the end of a race. One form of training that prepares athletes for this is where the coach requires them to do very fast runs between which there is a very short rest. Thus the athlete is expected to perform with great amounts of lactic acid in the muscle, incurring what is known as 'oxygen debt'. Eventually the athlete manages to cope with this anaerobic activity and the pain of the fatigue.

This is an arduous form of training even for experienced athletes and should not constitute the sole method of training.

Fartlek

This Scandinavian form of training is literally 'speed-play'. It places the onus on the athlete to decide when to place the effort and is best carried out over a country course which provides an interesting array of hills, fast stretches and rough ground. Though an experienced athlete will be able to 'push' himself to include more fast running stretches than slower ones, less experienced athletes might need direction. A coach or teacher could accompany his athletes, giving directions such as 'we will begin by jogging 800 metres'; 'now sprint 100 metres'; 'now jog 200 metres'; now walk down this hill'; 'now run as fast as possible to the end of this path'; 'now walk 200 metres'; 'now as fast as possible to the top of this hill'.

Resistance running

Arthur Lydiard in New Zealand, Percy Cerutty in Australia, Gundar Haegg in Sweden and Jim Alford in Wales all had something in common – the insistence on frequent hill-running as part of their athletes' training. Whether the hills are mud, snow, sand or coal seems not to matter provided athletes are required to run up them fast, using their arms vigorously, and repeat the runs often.

Other forms of resistance running include harness running, described on pages 21 and 23, running in heavy boots, running with sacks of sand on the back and running with weighted belts. Whenever a coach employs these methods

he should consider the objective, and whether the same effect could be obtained in another way. Sometimes coaches tend to become slaves to one method which has value only at limited periods during a year.

Weights and circuits

Weight training and circuit training are valuable forms of work for middle-distance runners and are fully described in *Conditioning for Sport* by this author (A&C Black, 1988).

Training – schedules

Devising schedules for middle-distance and cross-country runners is no easy task – they differ so much in capacity for work, physiological make-up, conscientiousness and occupation! An enthusiastic office-junior who has little talent will need different treatment from a farm labourer of similar age who has great potential but whose job leaves him less than willing to cover great distances on the track at the end of a day.

800 metres men (off-season, good standard athlete)

DAY 1 ▶	20 miles' (30km) road run
DAY 2 ▶	Run 800m on grass four times with a 3-minute interval between each run
DAY 3 ▶	5 miles' (8,000m) sustained run Weight training for arms and shoulders
DAY 4 ▶	Run 400m on the track in about 62 seconds Repeat eleven times, with a 2-minute recovery interval between each run
DAY 5 ▶	Fartlek for 45 minutes Harness running
DAY 6 ▶	6 miles' (10,000m) 'easy run'
DAY 7 ▶	Competition (cross-country) or Hard 45-minute Fartlek and weight training session

800 metres men (during season, good standard athlete)

DAY 1 ▶	30-minute Fartlek
DAY 2 ▶	Run 400m in under 58 seconds; repeat seven times Run 200m in under 28 seconds; repeat once Sprint 100m, fast; repeat once
DAY 3 ▶	Jog for 3 miles (5,000m) Run 1,200m at an even pace in about 3 minutes 15 seconds; repeat once Run 300m time trial
DAY 4 ▶	Run 600m in under 85 seconds Run 200m in under 26 seconds; repeat twice Sprint 100m in under 13 seconds; repeat five times
DAY 5 ▶	Run 200m ten times Run 400m twice Throughout these runs practise pace judgement, bearing the next competition in mind
DAY 6 ▶	Carry out usual pre-race-day routine. Some may rest, others do a steady jog over a short distance
DAY 7 ▶	Competition (400m, 800m or 1,500m)

800 metres women (off-season, good standard athlete)

DAY 1 ▶	8 miles' (12km) road run
DAY 2 ▶	Run 800m on grass four times, with a 4-minute interval between each run
DAY 3 ▶	3 miles' (5,000m) sustained run Weight training for arms and shoulders
DAY 4 ▶	Run 400m on the track ten to fifteen times with a 30 to 45-second interval between each run
DAY 5 ▶	Fartlek for 30 minutes Possibly some circuit-training
DAY 6 ▶	4 miles' (6,000m) 'easy run'
DAY 7 ▶	Competition (cross-country) or 30-minute Fartlek, or harness running

800 metres women   (during season, good standard athlete)

DAY 1 ▶	20-minute Fartlek
DAY 2 ▶	Run 400m in under 72 seconds; repeat four times Run 200m in under 35 seconds; repeat once Sprint 100m, fast; repeat once
DAY 3 ▶	Jog for 3,000m Run 1,000m, evenly paced; repeat once Run 300m time trial
DAY 4 ▶	Run 600m in under 105 seconds Run 200m in under 34 seconds; repeat twice Sprint 100m, fast; repeat three times
DAY 5 ▶	Run 200m six times Run 400m twice Throughout these runs practise pace judgement, bearing the next competition in mind
DAY 6 ▶	Carry out normal pre-race-day routine. Some athletes rest completely, others jog a short distance
DAY 7 ▶	Competition (400m, 800m or 1,500m)

1,500 metres men   (off-season, good standard athlete)

DAY 1 ▶	20 miles' (30km) road run
DAY 2 ▶	Run 1,600m on grass four times, with a 5-minute interval between each run
DAY 3 ▶	Hard 10,000m sustained run Weight training or circuit training
DAY 4 ▶	Run 400m in approximately 62–3 seconds; repeat fifteen times, with $1\frac{1}{2}$–2 minutes' recovery interval between each run
DAY 5 ▶	50 minutes' Fartlek or hill-running
DAY 6 ▶	8 miles' (12km) 'easy' run
DAY 7 ▶	Competition (cross-country) or Hard Fartlek, up to 1 hour

1,500 metres men (during season, good standard athlete)

DAY 1 ▶	1-hour Fartlek
DAY 2 ▶	Run 2,400m time trial Jog 2,400m Cover 100m using fast strides; repeat three times
DAY 3 ▶	Jog 4 miles (6,000m) Run 1,200m twice, with an even pace Run 400m fast
DAY 4 ▶	Sprint 200m in under 26 seconds; repeat three times Sprint 100m in under 13 seconds; repeat three times Sprint 400m in under 56 seconds; repeat once
DAY 5 ▶	Jog 2 miles (3,000m) Run 600m four times; practise pace judgement, bearing the next competition in mind
DAY 6 ▶	Carry out normal pre-race-day routine.
DAY 7 ▶	Competition (800m, 1,500m or 5,000m)

1,500 metres women (off-season, good standard athlete)

DAY 1 ▶	Up to 10 miles' (15km) road run
DAY 2 ▶	Run 1,600m on grass four times, with approximately 5 minutes' interval between each run
DAY 3 ▶	Hard 5,000m sustained run Circuit training
DAY 4 ▶	Run 400m fifteen to twenty times; repeat ten times, with a 45-second interval between each run
DAY 5 ▶	40 minutes' Fartlek or hill runs
DAY 6 ▶	6 miles' (10,000m) 'easy' run
DAY 7 ▶	Competition (cross-country) or Hard Fartlek, up to 45 minutes

1,500 metres women   (during season, good standard athlete)

DAY 1 ▶	30-minute Fartlek
DAY 2 ▶	Run 2,000m time trial Jog 2,000m Sprint 100m, fast, three times
DAY 3 ▶	Jog 3,000m Run 1,200m at an even pace; repeat once Run 400m fast
DAY 4 ▶	Run 200m in under 34 seconds; repeat twice Run 100m fast; repeat twice Run 400m in under 70 seconds; repeat once
DAY 5 ▶	Jog 2,000m Run 600m three times; practise pace judgement, bearing the next competition in mind
DAY 6 ▶	Carry out usual pre-race-day routine.
DAY 7 ▶	Competition (800m or 1,500m)

Cross-country and 5,000 metres (men)   (off-season)

DAY 1 ▶	20 miles' (30km) road run
DAY 2 ▶	1-hour Fartlek Weight training or circuit training
DAY 3 ▶	Interval or Tempo-training, e.g.: Run 1,000m once; run 800m twice; run 600m three times; run 400m four times
DAY 4 ▶	10-mile (15km) run (including hills, or possibly some resistance work or weight training)
DAY 5 ▶	Run 5 miles (7,500m) on grass or 6×800m with 1-minute jog interval
DAY 6 ▶	Carry out usual pre-race-day routine, or run for 30 minutes with a mixture of fast and slow running
DAY 7 ▶	Competition, or time trial, or Fartlek, or harness running, etc.

Cross-country and 5,000 metres runners (men) (during season)

DAY 1 ▶	1–2 hours' Fartlek
DAY 2 ▶	Run 400m in under 62 seconds; repeat eleven times, with 1½ minutes' recovery interval between each run Jog for 15 minutes Run 800m four times
DAY 3 ▶	6 miles' (10,000m) hard sustained run
DAY 4 ▶	Run 1,200m at 5,000m racing speed twice, with 10 minutes' jogging between runs Run 600m eight times
DAY 5 ▶	Stride quickly over distances of 200m for 10 minutes Jog for 10 minutes Run 400m fast; repeat five times Run 200m fast; repeat five times
DAY 6 ▶	Carry out usual pre-race-day routine
DAY 7 ▶	Competition (1,500m–10,000 metres)

Cross-country and 3,000 metres runners (women)
(off-season)

DAY 1 ▶	10 miles' (15km) road run
DAY 2 ▶	45-minutes' Fartlek. Weights or circuit training
DAY 3 ▶	Run 800m once; run 600m twice; run 400m three times; run 200m four times
DAY 4 ▶	6 miles' (10,000m) road run including hills
DAY 5 ▶	Run 3 miles (5,000m) on grass
DAY 6 ▶	Carry out usual pre-race-day routine, or run for 15 minutes with a mixture of fast and slow running
DAY 7 ▶	Competition, or time trial, or Fartlek, or harness running

Cross-country and 3,000 metres runners (women)
(during season)

DAY 1 ▶	1-hour Fartlek
DAY 2 ▶	Run 400m under 75 seconds; repeat five times, with 2 minutes' recovery interval between each run Jog/walk for 15 minutes Run 600m four times
DAY 3 ▶	3,000m hard sustained run
DAY 4 ▶	Run 800m at racing speed twice, with 15 minutes' jogging between runs Run 600m, when the pulse rate drops to 120 beats per minute run 500m, then 400m, then 300m, then 200m
DAY 5 ▶	Stride quickly over distances of 200m for 10 minutes Jog for 10 minutes Run 300m fast; repeat three times Run 150m fast; repeat three times
DAY 6 ▶	Carry out usual pre-race-day routine
DAY 7 ▶	Competition (800m–3,000m)

All that can be provided here are mere guidelines, and intelligent teachers and coaches will adapt them to suit the ages, abilities, sex and disposition of their own athletes. It will be noticed that in some cases two sessions per day are noted; these are for better athletes. In fact, some internationals train three times per day with a long run before breakfast, a session at lunch-time and a further session in the evening. They have spent a number of years building up to this, so one good session should suffice for beginners. The important thing to remember is that variety is a prerequisite to improvement.

Rules

The usual track rules apply but middle-distance runners should comply with the following in particular.

(a) Refreshments are not to be provided in races of 10 miles (15km) or less.
(b) Competitors taking drugs will be liable to disqualification.

(c) Competitors must at once retire from a race if ordered to do so by a member of the official medical staff.
(d) Numbers must be worn on the chest.
(e) Clothing must be made of a material which is not transparent when wet.
(f) No person other than the official time-keepers shall indicate 'lap times' to athletes.
(g) Starting blocks are *not* permitted in races of 800 metres and over.
(h) Any competitor who jostles, runs across or obstructs another athlete so that his progress is affected shall be liable to disqualification.
(i) Athletes who voluntarily leave the track or course shall not be allowed to continue in the race.

STEEPLECHASE

The steeplechase event in the Olympic Games is a 3,000 metres race on the track during which the athlete has to clear hurdles twenty-eight times and a water jump seven times. It is therefore a most arduous race demanding endurance, skill, courage and tactical planning.

The athlete

Past steeplechasers have been either cross-country runners who use this as their summer event 'to keep fit', or runners who have been converted from middle distances.

Seven water jumps and twenty-eight hurdles have to be cleared in the 3,000m steeplechase, making it one of the toughest track events

Steeplechasers need to be good distance runners with good hurdle clearance technique and a vast amount of courage and determination

The steeplechase hurdle

Nowadays steeplechase specialists have emerged, and those who arrive via one of the above-mentioned routes soon discover that it is not an easy event, and that the standards at top-class level are very high.

Steeplechasing has also appeared in schools in recent years, though boys run either 2,000 or 1,500m, dependent upon their age. It is not a recognised women's event, neither is it recommended for them.

No particular body type succeeds in steeplechase, but it is a tough event needing the middle-distance runner's endurance and determination, and the hurdler's skill and versatility.

Equipment

● No personal equipment additional to the needs of a middle-distance runner is required, except that the rule forbidding the wearing of transparent shorts relates particularly to steeplechasers, who tend to get wet during the race!

● The steeplechase hurdles are different from the usual track race hurdles. Steeplechase hurdles are of solid construction because athletes do not have to hurdle them; if they wish they may step on to them. They are 91·4cm high and 3·66m wide.

The water jump

Fig 7 Usual layout for the steeplechase

USUAL LAYOUT

Measurements are as follows:

Start to beginning
of first full lap
(No jumping or hurdling)   242m

From beginning of first
full lap to 1st hurdle   15.80m

1st hurdle to 2nd hurdle   79m
2nd hurdle to 3rd hurdle   79m
3rd hurdle to water jump   79m

Water jump to 4th hurdle   62.20m

4th hurdle to finish line   79m

7 full laps are run, making total distance 3,000m

Progressive stages

● The water jump is 3·66m long and the same width. The water is 70cm deep, tapering off the level of the track at the end away from the hurdle.

The track can have the water jump placed in a number of positions, as illustrated in Figs 7 and 8.

1. First, the intending steeplechaser needs to be soundly fit, and to have had his endurance developed over a long period of time by the practices described in the chapter on middle-distance and cross-country running.
2. Secondly, the intending steeplechaser needs

Fig 8 Alternative layouts for the steeplechase

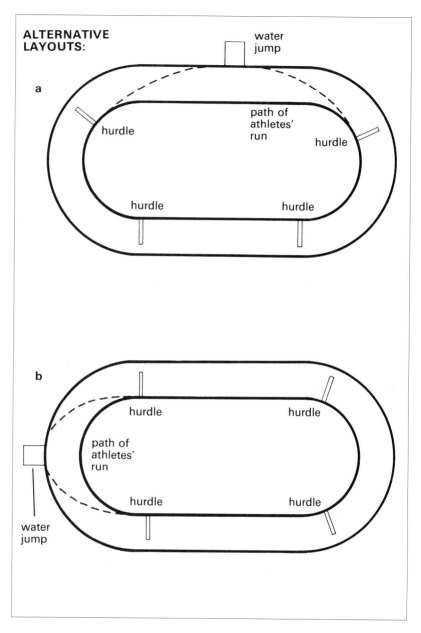

ALTERNATIVE LAYOUTS:

a

water jump

hurdle

path of athletes' run

hurdle

hurdle

hurdle

b

hurdle

hurdle

path of athletes' run

hurdle

hurdle

water jump

to have developed a good hurdling technique over a 3ft (91·4cm) high barrier. This will have been acquired over a period of time in practices described in the chapter on hurdles.
3. Additional practice must be given for the water jump technique. This will be done first of all by getting the athlete to run, step on a steeplechase hurdle, and continue running a short distance. Effort will be applied on top of the hurdle so that the athlete will be driving forward as far away from the hurdle as possible.
4. Having acquired proficiency at driving off a steeplechase hurdle, the next stage is to carry out the same practice at the water jump hurdle, but with no water in the water jump; at the learner stage, the athlete will not be driving

Above **Practising the step on to the hurdle**

Right **Practising the drive off the hurdle**

This athlete keeps his centre of gravity low as he steps on to the water jump hurdle

Driving for the far end of the water jump

Better steeplechasers save time and energy by *hurdling* over the hurdles – but not over the water jump!

The athlete in this photograph wastes much time and energy by jumping over every obstacle

sufficiently far off the hurdle.

5. The final beginner stage is the use of a check mark a short distance before the water jump, so that the athlete can arrange his feet in such a way that he can be running fast at the water jump hurdle.

Then comes the point at which the athlete must be able to run laps, in each of which four hurdles and a water jump are included.

Training

During the winter, steeplechasers will train with a mixture of cross-country racing, middle-distance running, and occasional hurdling.

During the summer, steeplechasers will continue a middle-distance runner's programme, adding hurdling and water jump techniques on one or two days, depending upon the runner's level of skill.

Rules

(a) Every competitor must go over or through the water at the water jump.
(b) Every competitor must go over every hurdle by hurdling, jumping or vaulting over them. He may place a foot on each hurdle.
(c) The usual rules for middle-distance events also apply.

WALKING RACES

'Walking is progression by steps so taken that unbroken contact with the ground is maintained. At each step, the advancing foot of the walker must make contact with the ground before the rear foot leaves the ground.' (IAAF Rule 191)

Above **This illustrates a very good 'legal' walking style. The back toe does not break contact with the ground until the front heel touches**

Right **Here the walker demonstrates an 'illegal' style, and would be disqualified. His rear foot is off the floor before the front foot is grounded**

Many people regard walking competitions as 'artificial' events; they would contend that if someone wished to get from A to B in a hurry, he would run. Many also regard walking races as a hilarious form of activity to observe, for the strange style of hip-wiggling and arm action tends to bring mirth to the faces of those who know little about race-walking.

Race-walkers defend their sport with a number of points. Firstly, they would point to the 'artificiality' of pole-vaulting, hammer-throwing and even the crouch start in sprinting. They would claim that in fact walking is a very natural activity, and that the style racers adopt is merely the result of man applying his brain to the task of making walking more efficient within the rules laid down. Secondly, they would emphasise the health aspect of walking, and the fact that it can be cheap with no special equipment or clothing needed. Thirdly, they would point out that Olympic competition is available for walkers, whereas it is not, for instance, for caber-tossing, and so walkers have world records and championships for which to strive. Finally, walkers would remind their critics that their sport can be continued throughout life, over different terrain, by men and women and children. In fact they would stress that throughout the world the best walkers tend to be well into their thirties, thus making the Olympic Games a balance between younger competitors (e.g. in swimming) and older competitors.

What about the unbiased teacher or coach who is considering whether or not he should introduce race-walking as an additional event in the school or club? There seem to be a number of considerations. Are there opportunities for competition locally, or not too far away? If the only competition is likely to be against one's fellow athletes or pupils, boredom may well set in, whereas if competition against other clubs or schools can be easily organised, there is an incentive for training.

Another consideration is judging. If there are no qualified judges, or people who can interpret the rules intelligently, then race-walking for beginners can become a disguised run, and a tendency to cheat can creep in.

Furthermore, if the club or school has a wide range of events and sports that seem to cater for all of the people, then it may well be that the time to introduce race-walking has not arrived.

But if a group of children or athletes shows interest in walking, and if they are not achieving success in other events, teachers and coaches should seriously consider introducing walking, and then secure the necessary judges and competitions to satisfy the established need.

The athlete

No particular body types succeed more than others in race-walking, that is if it is taken for granted that the obese and the very weak are unlikely to be successful. International 'stars' have included Olympic gold medallist Don Thompson, a very small, light-framed individual who wore spectacles, and who in his normal clothes would not have impressed any onlooker as being the layman's idea of a world-class athlete. Another Olympic gold medal winner, Ken Matthews, was very tall and muscular and could have been mistaken for a top-class high jumper or hurdler.

One generalisation about race-walkers can be made, however. They must build up their strength and endurance with walking, running, exercises and weights, because race-walking is a very demanding activity that puts a strain on all muscle groups. In view of the fact that walking races tend to be over longer distances, athletes should be well-prepared over a period of time before they are entered for competitions. Walkers tend to suffer from leg problems such as 'shin splints', that is pain in the front of the legs. These are often due to weakness and can be overcome gradually as the athlete grows stronger. During a race the pain can only be relieved by slowing down, and similarly in training it is better not to stop altogether, but to 'walk out' the pain. Another problem that arises is at the knee joint, on to which the body-weight is forced in the normal walking style. Some athletes are unable to lock the knee during the walk due to weakness. As the strength increases, and exercises stretch the ligaments, the knee problems tend to disappear.

Surprising as it may seem, some walkers also suffer from abdominal pains. This is often due

Eyes looking forward, vigorous arm action and one foot always in contact with the ground – these are the essentials of good walking to weakness in the stomach muscles and in time the pain lessens. Sometimes, however, the pain is the result of a bad trunk position, and the style needs attention. In addition, the usual breathing difficulties such as 'stitch' appear in walking. A good warm-up before the race, no heavy meals before the race, and an improvement in fitness will tend to alleviate breathing problems.

To summarise, one could say that, like all athletics events, race-walking needs careful preparation, hard training, good food, helpful coaching and dedication. There is a great deal of skill required, but not of the nature of the flexible pole-vaulting skill, for instance. Race-walking can suit a large number of people who would not otherwise take part in athletics, but it is not an easy event, to be taken lightly. Teachers, coaches, athletes and schoolchildren should ensure that race-walking receives the adequate preparation which would be given to any other athletics event.

Equipment

● At an early stage, strong shoes, training shoes or strong plimsolls are adequate. Blisters tend to be a problem for walkers; in time the athlete will be able to discern which shoes and socks and foot powders suit him best, and he will ensure that new footwear is well 'broken in' before being used in competition.
● For winter training, track suits or warm clothes will be necessary to protect muscles from injury. During cold weather competition, long sleeves and gloves can be an asset, whereas in very hot climates 'aertex' vests will be worn. To summarise, it is sufficient to say that a minimum of clothing and equipment is necessary for race-walking, and athletes will soon select those items that give greatest comfort and efficiency.

Race-walking techniques

At the beginning, children or athletes will be under the impression that walking is easy. Within minutes, it will become apparent that

This athlete prefers to wear his vest outside his shorts to allow fresh air to reach his midriff. He also dispenses with socks in races up to 10,000 metres. For races above that distance, and in dusty conditions, he finds value in wearing socks. Athletes each have their own preference

When the pressure is on there is a tendency to 'lift', that is to have both feet off the ground at once. Umpires are spread around the track to disqualify anyone breaking the rules

walking in races requires about a one-third increase in stride length, a considerable increase in hip-rotation, a very vigorous arm action and a changed foot/leg angle. All of this convinces the beginner that an analysis is necessary to ensure the greater efficiency which will make the race-walking less of an effort. Because we tend to think mainly of the legs as the propulsive force in race-walking, the leg action will be considered first.

Leg action

The race-walking rules require that the knee of the leading leg is straight when it reaches the vertical position, and that the heel of the leading leg touches the ground before the rear foot leaves the ground. Therefore a good technique must be developed in the early stages, not only to ensure that there is no waste of effort, but also to ensure that a legal style is learned.

Beginners tend to find the legal style a strain, particularly at the knees, and they tend to slap the front foot down. In fact the heel of the leading leg should reach the ground first with the knee practically straight, but with the thigh muscles relaxed. As soon as contact with the ground is made, the muscles tighten and a pulling action begins which straightens the leg.

During this time the rear leg remains straight as long as possible to keep the body going at speed. Thus we have a pulling effect from the front leg and a pushing effect from the rear leg. But this effective propulsion depends on correct foot action. The rear foot must not leave the ground until the drive is continued right up to the point of the toe. Beginners raise their rear leg when the ball of the foot is on the ground, thus losing almost 8cm of stride length. As the aim is to obtain a stride length of about 1·2m (for adults), and as the good walkers take about three strides every second, the rear foot must drive right up on to the toe.

Here the walker demonstrates excellent arm drive, relaxation and stride length

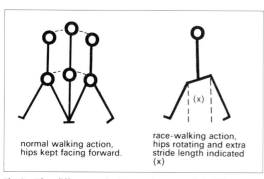

normal walking action, hips kept facing forward.

race-walking action, hips rotating and extra stride length indicated (x)

Fig 9   The differences between the normal walking action and the race-walking technique

A rear view of a good walking style in which the athlete drives up on to the back toe while making contact first with the heel in front

The front heel will land first and a smooth transition is made on to the ball of the foot, with a drive off the inside ball of the foot area, finishing off with the toe. Some tend to use a splay-foot style to gain extra distance; this is permissible provided that the swinging-through action concentrates on a toe-pointing-forward movement, and not a wasteful rotated foot action.

Hip action

When the speed of normal walking increases, one tends to rotate the hips so that the stride length and speed increase. Additionally there is a lowering of the body as illustrated. In race-walking the hips swing forward and also one side is elevated higher than the other. This is automatic and needs no undue emphasis

Vigorous use of the arms is essential, as demonstrated by the walkers in the front

in coaching. The gain in stride length from this hip movement can be as much as 20cm. The elimination of the body raising and lowering conserves energy.

Head and trunk positions

Holding the head too far forward creates extra muscle tension and cuts down the rotation of the hips, thus shortening the stride length. Holding the head too far back causes extra effort, uses up energy wastefully and shortens the stride. As in running events, the ideal head position is in natural alignment with the body, with the eyes gazing forwards down the track (not immediately in front of the feet, and not up into the sky).

The best trunk position is a vertical one. Any undue tendency to lean forward or back will adversely affect the performance. There are occasions, however, when there is a need to make adjustments to the head and trunk. When walking up hills a slight lean forward will be necessary; this will facilitate the hip action. Downhill walking needs particular attention to avoid disqualification; a slight lean backwards will assist in slowing down the speed of the walk which otherwise might become a run.

Arm action

As in running events, the arm action is of considerably more importance than people generally believe. The race-walking arm style should emphasise relaxed shoulders and bent elbows. The arm in front will tend to come across the chest and the rear arm will drive backwards with the elbow at an angle of about 90°, but this angle changes throughout the forward and backward drive and should not be held mechanically always at the same angle.

At this point it is useful to recall that, as in other events, there is no **one** ideal style. Athletes differ in their body structure; their arms (and leg) levers are therefore different, and consequently styles will differ slightly.

Nevertheless, one must guard against a tiring, wasteful arm action, and against a shoulder/arm action that will tend to lift the feet off the floor. The hands are usually quite relaxed, playing little part in the drive. It must be remembered that an emphasis on arm drive can occasionally enable walkers with tired legs to increase speed. It is important, therefore, to adopt a good arm style that can contribute to the drive forwards, prevent lifting of the feet, and assist in the hip-rotation process.

The two front walkers are unnecessarily 'getting their heads down', which will in fact reduce their stride length and slow them down. The two rear walkers are looking well ahead, but are too stiff and jerky in their style to overtake relaxed walkers

Training

For beginners, short distances are recommended: hikes, time trials, relay races, team races, etc. The emphasis should be on fun, adhering to the rules, getting used to the technique of race-walking, and avoiding the temptation to run.

When teachers or coaches are convinced that the athletes are ready for planned training, a systematic programme can be prepared. During the early stages the emphasis will be on correct technique, with the coach ensuring that the distances covered are not so long that the skill factor breaks down.

Juniors

As children gain experience, the teacher or coach can check for the ten main faults at least once a week.

Faults:

1. placing the front foot down flat
2. placing the front foot down sideways
3. leg not straight at the knee
4. over-striding
3. under-striding
6. over-emphasis of the hip swing
7. the centre of gravity of the body bouncing up and down during the walk
8. shoulder shrugging
9. leaning forwards with head or trunk
10. leaning backwards with head or trunk.

The checking and correction of these faults should be done with the coach standing well away from the athlete, and observing his progress from the side, front and back. Additionally, winter training can include circuit training, weight training and endurance running on the track and over country courses.

Seniors

It can be assumed that those walkers who continue training beyond the junior stage are sufficiently well-motivated to wish to train daily with a variety of types of work. A hard programme can therefore be planned, with the assurance that there has been a progressively developed style and background of fitness training. The next stage of training can be specifically designed to eradicate the athlete's weaknesses and at the same time prepare him for the more energy-sapping long-distance races.

Beginner schoolchildren   (off-season)

DAY 1 ▶	Cover 3 miles (5,000m) with a mixture of walking and jogging, with the emphasis on style
DAY 2 ▶	No walking
DAY 3 ▶	On track or school field, walk 600m twice; walk 400m twice; walk 200m twice
DAY 4 ▶	No walking
DAY 5 ▶	Races with fellow pupils, relays, team races, etc.

Beginner schoolchildren   (during season)

DAY 1 ▶	Walk 2 miles (3,000m) using three-quarters effort
DAY 2 ▶	No walking
DAY 3 ▶	Walk 600m, rest; walk 500m, rest; walk 400m, rest; walk 300m, rest; walk 200m, rest; walk 100m
DAY 4 ▶	No walking
DAY 5 ▶	Cover 3 miles (5,000m) with a mixture of walking and jogging
DAY 6 ▶	No walking
DAY 7 ▶	Competition; 1,600m or 3,000m

Older schoolchildren   (off-season)

DAY 1 ▶	Cover 5 miles (8,000m) with a mixture of fast and slow walking and jogging
DAY 2 ▶	Walk 2 miles (3,000m), using three-quarters effort
DAY 3 ▶	Walk 800m twice; walk 400m three times; walk 200m four times
DAY 4 ▶	Walk 4 miles (6,000m) at a steady pace
DAY 5 ▶	No walking
DAY 6 ▶	Competition: 3,000m or 5,000m

Older schoolchildren (during season)

DAY 1 ▶	Cover 6 miles (10,000m) with a mixture of fast and slow walking and jogging
DAY 2 ▶	Walk 3 miles (5,000m) at a steady pace
DAY 3 ▶	Walk 400m fast; walk 200m slow; walk 400m fast; walk 200m slow Repeat sequence twice
DAY 4 ▶	Walk 4 miles (6,000m) at a steady pace
DAY 5 ▶	No walking
DAY 6 ▶	Competition: 3,000m or 5,000m

Junior walkers (off-season)

DAY 1 ▶	Walk 8 miles (12km) at a steady pace
DAY 2 ▶	Do weight training or circuit training
DAY 3 ▶	5-mile (8,000m) Fartlek, including fast and slow walks and jogging
DAY 4 ▶	Walk 3 miles (5,000m) fast
DAY 5 ▶	Track running: run 800m twice; run 600m twice; run 400m twice
DAY 6 ▶	Walk 6 miles (10,000m) working on technique
DAY 7 ▶	Rest day

Junior walkers (during season)

DAY 1 ▶	Walk 6 miles (10,000m) at a steady pace
DAY 2 ▶	Walk 4 miles (6,000m) with a mixture of fast and slow walking
DAY 3 ▶	Walk 1,000m five times
DAY 4 ▶	Walk 3 miles (5,000m) fast
DAY 5 ▶	Walk 800m twice; walk 600m twice; walk 400m twice; walk 200m twice
DAY 6 ▶	Rest day
DAY 7 ▶	Competition

Senior walkers   (off-season)

DAY 1 ▶	Walk 15–20 miles (25–30km) across country and/or road
DAY 2 ▶	Do weight training or circuit training
DAY 3 ▶	Fartlek (cross-country running, fast and slow)
DAY 4 ▶	Walk using three-quarters effort for 2 hours
DAY 5 ▶	Short walk (30 minutes) plus weight training
DAY 6 ▶	Rest from walking (play games, basketball, badminton, etc.)
DAY 7 ▶	Competition or time trial

Senior walkers   (during season)

DAY 1 ▶	Walk for 3 hours, using three-quarters effort
DAY 2 ▶	Run 200m eight times. Possibly some weight training
DAY 3 ▶	Walk 1,600m twice; walk 1,200m twice; walk 800m twice; walk 400m twice
DAY 4 ▶	Walk for 2 hours at a steady pace
DAY 5 ▶	Walk 600m three times; walk 400m three times; walk 200m three times; walk 100m three times fast
DAY 6 ▶	30 minutes' jogging and stretching exercises
DAY 7 ▶	Competition or time trial

The athlete will be expected to warm-up well before each daily session; to work daily on mobility exercises that will make him more supple in the joints and less tense in the muscles; to work hard on advanced weight-training techniques to improve his strength; to use circuit training as an indication of improvement in his muscular endurance; and to improve his speed by training over shorter distances than his race distance whilst ensuring that his style is legal.

One of the important features of advanced training is that there should be plenty of variety to relieve the boredom of the constant hard work. This can be achieved by ensuring a mixture of track, road and country work, a mixture of indoor and outdoor work, a constant change of environment, a regular change of the distances covered and, most important of all, an assurance that the work is progressively more difficult, of greater volume and related to an athlete's improved strength and endurance as the year progresses.

Additionally, an advanced athlete will take greater care of his leisure hours, i.e. no smoking, no alcohol, no late nights, a good diet, meticulous care and cleanliness of clothing and body, and regular medical checks. In view of the long distances covered, particular attention should be paid to diet, bearing in mind the possible need for supplementary foods, drinks, vitamins – all in conjunction with medical advice and not taken because of a whim or a belief that patent medicines can improve performance.

The advanced walkers will also consider the need for sustenance during their races, and will experiment with different drinks and foods during their training period, to ensure that on racing days they eat or drink only those substances in which they have confidence.

At this stage of an athlete's career he will be less inclined to want to take a few days' rest should he have a sports injury. The treatment of sports injuries is not always the family doctor's province; in fact the athlete himself can often educate the doctor about specific injuries related to his own event. Nevertheless, advanced walkers should be working in co-operation with family doctors and, where available, sports injuries specialists. Where there is an injury, some form of training can still be done – avoiding the particular muscle area in which the injury is present.

Tactics

It is useful to plan races taking into account an athlete's present level of fitness, his strengths, his target (i.e. the position expected in the race, or a time), the opposition's strengths, weaknesses and abilities, and the nature of the course and weather.

Unlike runners, walkers get no benefit from being shielded from the wind by walking behind someone else, neither is it always possible or advisable to change speed or put in spurts during the race. Such action is wasteful of energy and can lead to disqualification if illegal 'lifting' of the feet results. It is therefore important that a walker knows his own ability and learns to appreciate at what speed he is walking at any time. Opponents might try to walk as fast as possible immediately the race begins; if an athlete attempts to match this, he

could 'burn himself up'. Surprisingly, if he decides not to go off with the fast bunch at the start, but retains a speed he knows he can cope with, he might well be overtaking the others at a later point during the race when they become tired.

Nevertheless, it is useful during training to try a number of different speeds and speed changes to discover whether they suit the individual. It may well be that some walkers will discover that they are good uphill walkers; they will therefore ensure that they obtain maximum advantage from the uphill stages of a race. The psychological factor is also very important. Walkers should not be tempted to change their own styles or plans because of the performance of others. Changing of style or effort can lead to disqualification, especially in the latter stages of a race.

Rules

(a) Athletes must progress in such a way that unbroken contact with the ground be maintained.
(b) The Chief Judge plus one other judge may disqualify a competitor if the style of walking does not comply with the rules.
(c) A walker may be given one caution if his walking style is not a valid one.
(d) On disqualification the competitor must immediately leave the track, or in a road race remove his number.
(e) Refreshments shall be provided in races of more than 20km at the 10km point and every 5km thereafter.

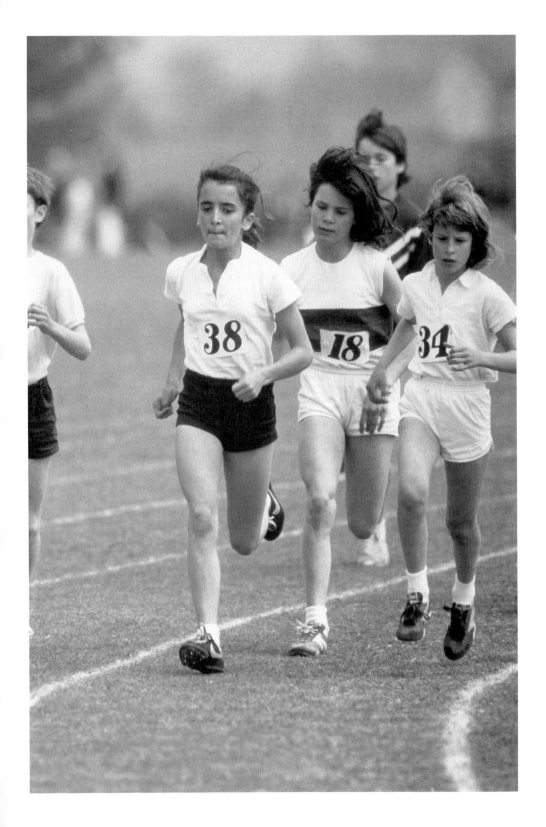

CONCLUDING DISCUSSION

Errors, like straws, upon the surface flow,
He who would search for pearls, must dive
                              below.
                              John Dryden

Progress

In a technological age, progress is very rapid: there are new techniques, new types of equipment, new physiological research findings, new temptations and even new ways of cheating!

This text was not prepared with the sole aim of producing better performances from track athletes. It is intented to act as a guide to building up practices which will ensure that young people enjoy learning skills presented to them in a purposeful fashion. It is very important that those responsible for young people in their care are concerned with the *full* development of the athlete.

Too often athletes are seen as individuals who must be moulded into a particular style and who must adhere to particular schedules. Good teachers and coaches teach the individual and *not* the athletics event.

Athletics is a sport which contains many events, all of which require considerable knowledge of coaching and also of precise organisation because of the dangers that exist. Therefore, the individual who chooses to teach or coach the sport must show a level of concern for young people. This concern should extend to ensuring that athletics is enjoyable, and that young people are not introduced to unhealthy or unfair practices.

The needs of children

Good physical education teachers and sports coaches will need to understand the requirements of children at different stages of physiological and psychological growth. They should also keep up to date with ongoing research into child development and take into account the opportunities that exist within the child's community.

APPENDIX A

Standard attainments to be attempted by schoolgirls

Girls' sprints and hurdles

	100 metres	200 metres	400 metres	Hurdles
Under 13 years	14·6 sec	31·7 sec	—	14·2 sec (70m)
Under 14 years	14·3 sec	30·5 sec	—	13·8 sec (70m)
Under 15 years	14·1 sec	29·6 sec	—	14·1 sec (75m)
Under 16 years	13·9 sec	29·4 sec	73·5 sec	15·5 sec (80m)
Under 17 years	13·7 sec	29·1 sec	72·3 sec	14·6 sec (80m)
Under 18 years	13·5 sec	29·0 sec	71·5 sec	19·8 sec (100m)

Girls' middle-distance and cross-country

	800 metres	1,500 metres	Cross-country distance
Under 13 years	2 min 57 sec	6 min 6 sec	
Under 14 years	2 min 52 sec	5 min 56 sec	Approximately 3,500 metres
Under 15 years	2 min 50 sec	5 min 56 sec	
Under 16 years	2 min 47 sec	5 min 52 sec	Approximately 4,000 metres
Under 17 years	2 min 45 sec	5 min 50 sec	
Under 18 years	2 min 40 sec	5 min 48 sec	Approximately 4,500 metres

The publication of 'standard' tables, though of value to schoolteachers, can be a cause for concern. They can give the impression that the teacher's own school is falling behind the level of progress of other schools or, alternatively, they may show that the school is ahead, thus encouraging the teacher to rest on his laurels.

The standards should therefore be regarded simply as guides. Should there be an athletics club in the vicinity of the school, it is likely that some of the pupils will join, thus affecting the 'average' scores. Standard tables remind teachers of those events which they may be neglecting.

Appendix B

Standard attainments to be attempted by schoolboys

Boys' sprints and hurdles

	100 metres	200 metres	400 metres	Hurdles
Under 13 years	14·2 sec	30·3 sec	68·4 sec	13·3 sec (70m)
Under 14 years	13·4 sec	28·8 sec	65·0 sec	13·0 sec (70m)
Under 15 years	12·7 sec	26·9 sec	61·1 sec	14·6 sec (80m)
Under 16 years	12·4 sec	26·2 sec	59·8 sec	17·0 sec (100m)
Under 17 years	12·1 sec	25·5 sec	58·5 sec	16·5 sec (100m)
Under 18 years	12·0 sec	25·2 sec	58·2 sec	19·5 sec (110m)

Boys' middle-distance and steeplechase

	800 metres	1,500 metres	3,000 metres	Steeplechase
Under 13 years	2 min 41 sec	5 min 28 sec	—	—
Under 14 years	2 min 33 sec	5 min 19 sec	—	—
Under 15 years	2 min 27 sec	5 min 05 sec	—	—
Under 16 years	2 min 22 sec	4 min 57 sec	—	6 min (1,500m)
Under 17 years	2 min 18 sec	4 min 49 sec	—	5 min 50 sec (1,500m)
Under 18 years	2 min 15 sec	4 min 45 sec	10 min 30 sec	7 min 30 sec (2,000m)

Cross-country
Because of the different terrain included on different courses, no standard times are suggested, but the distances run should be as follows:
Aged 13 & 14 – under 5,000 metres
Aged 15 & 16 – under 6,500 metres
Aged 17 & 18 – under 8,000 metres

The range of events available for schoolboys to attempt depends on a number of factors, including:
(a) the facilities available,
(b) the equipment available,
(c) an interest in athletics in the locality of the school and
(d) the teacher's own interests.

The more events offered in the school's curriculum, the more each boy is likely to find some event which interests him or suits his ability. However, since track events are not ideal for all physiques and abilities, the school should also introduce field events to its pupils.

Appendix C

Standards for schoolchildren in athletics clubs

Targets for schoolgirls in athletics clubs (i.e. additional coaching outside school)

	100 metres	200 metres	400 metres	800 metres	Hurdles
Aged 13 & 14	13·4 sec	27·5 sec	—	2 min 35 sec	13·0 sec (75m)
Aged 15 & 16	13·2 sec	26·6 sec	65 sec	2 min 30 sec	12·6 sec (80m)
Aged 17 & 18	13·0 sec	25·8 sec	60 sec	2 min 26 sec	15·5 sec (100m)
Aged 19	12·8 sec	25·4 sec	58 sec	2 min 20 sec	15·2 sec (100m)

Targets for schoolboys in athletics clubs

	100 metres	200 metres	400 metres	Hurdles
Aged 13 & 14	12·6 sec	25·8 sec	59·0 sec	13·6 sec (80m)
Aged 15 & 16	11·9 sec	23·9 sec	54·3 sec	15·4 sec (100m)
Aged 17 & 18	11·6 sec	23·6 sec	53·5 sec	17·0 sec (110m)
Aged 19	11·3 sec	23·1 sec	52·0 sec	16·4 sec (110m)

	800 metres	1,500 metres	5,000 metres	Steeplechase
Aged 13 & 14	2 min 19 sec	4 min 42 sec	—	—
Aged 15 & 16	2 min 05 sec	4 min 18 sec	—	5 min (1,500m)
Aged 17 & 18	2 mins	4 min 10 sec	15 min 30 sec	10 min 20 sec (3,000m)
Aged 19	1 min 56 sec	4 min	15 min	9 min 50 sec (3,000m)

Athletics clubs perform an important function. In addition to forming a link between schools and top level competition, they are able often to provide access to events and coaching expertise not available in schools.

In the atmosphere of an athletics club, where those attending are concentrating on one event with a view to future competition, higher standards of achievement may be expected of schoolchildren compared with children from schools which are not located near to an athletics clubs. Teachers have to accept that the main objective in athletics clubs is to win, whereas in schools it may be simply to enjoy taking part.

APPENDIX D

Standards for walkers

(The walks events are arduous, and coaches will ensure that athletes are well-prepared before they undergo time trials. The following are very approximate and depend upon previous training and the surfaces walked upon.)

Boys	1,000 metres	2,000 metres	3,000 metres
Aged 13, 14, 15	5 min	11 min	17 min
Aged 16, 17	4 min 40 sec	10 min 30 sec	16 min
Aged 18, 19	4 min 20 sec	10 min	15 min

Girls	1,000 metres	2,000 metres	3,000 metres
Aged 13, 14, 15	7 min 10 sec	15 min 50 sec	18 min 50 secs
Aged 16, 17	6 min 40 sec	14 min	18 min
Aged 18, 19	5 min	12 min	17 min

COMPETITION

Recommended distances:

	Boys	Girls
Aged 12, 13, 14	3,000 metres	2,500 metres
Aged 15, 16	5,000 metres	3,000 metres
Aged 17, 18, 19	10,000 metres	5,000 metres

With 'Cinderella' events such as walking, it is always difficult firstly to motivate children to participate and secondly to maintain their interest.

Standards in the sport of walking, as in other athletics events, could be set at different levels. Thus the above standards could be the 'gold award', a lesser standard could be a 'silver award', while a standard attainable by all could be called a 'bronze award'.

FURTHER INFORMATION

Books
British Amateur Athletic Board, *How To Organise an Athletics Meeting* (BAAB)
British Amateur Athletic Board, *Know the Game Track and Field Athletics* (A&C Black, 1986)
Department of Education and Science, *Physical Education in Schools, 5–16* (HMSO)
Dick, F., *Sports Training Principles* (A&C Black, 1989)
Dyson, G., *Mechanics of Athletics* (University of London Press, 1978)
English Schools' Athletics Association, *Handbook*
International Amateur Athletic Federation, *Athletics Officiating* (IAAF)
Johnson, C., *Skilful Field Athletics* (A&C Black, 1990)
Paish, W., *Diet in Sport* (A&C Black, 1989)
Whitehead, N., *Conditioning for Sport* (A&C Black, 1988)
Whitehead, N. and Cook, M., *Soccer Training* (A&C Black, 1988)

Films
BOA Film Library, Pottery Lave, London W11 4LZ
IAAF Films, 162 Upper Richmond Road, London SW15
GRE Films, Guild of Sound & Vision, Peterborough

Magazines
Athletics Weekly, 344 High Street, Rochester, Kent ME1 1DT

USEFUL ADDRESSES

Athletic Congress of the United States of America
PO Box 120
Indianapolis
Indiana 462060120
United States of America

British Amateur Athletic Board
Edgbaston House
3 Duchess Place
Hagley Road
Edgbaston
Birmingham B16 8NM
Tel: 021 456 4050

International Amateur Athletic Federation
3 Hans Crescent
Knightsbridge
London SW1X 0LN

The Sports Council Information Centre
16 Upper Woburn Place
London WC1H 0QP
Tel: 01 388 1277

Women's Amateur Athletic Association
Secretary: Miss M. Hartman CBE
             Women's Amateur Athletic
             Association
             Francis House
             Francis Street
             London SW1P 1DL
             Tel: 01 828 9326

INDEX

78   9

The Library,
Worcester College of Higher Education,
Henwick Grove, WORCESTER.

.ne Peirson Library
'TY COLLEGE WORCESTER

A16044